"Friendships in many circles are a lost art. A fast-paced, driven world that urges us to care for ourselves does not push us together but rather pushes us apart. God has designed us to do life together with others. Jerry and Mary White have years of real-life experience with friends they've walked with for a lifetime. Their lives are a testimony of how friendships can set us up for flourishing lives. In a lonely world, friendships are standard equipment for living joyfully, through thick and thin, as God has designed us to live. Don't miss this time-tested wisdom."

—DR. DOUG NUENKE, president, The Navigators (U.S.)

"Jerry and Mary just tripled my understanding about the richness and diversities of true friendship! Generously they open the curtain on their friendships and let us in on the fun, the sadness, and their memorable stories. *To Be a Friend* is packed with gems, plus dozens of poignant quotations on friendship I'm already sharing with my friends."

—JOHN PEARSON, author of *Mastering the Management Buckets*

"What it means to be a friend has changed quickly over the past fifteen years. Jerry and Mary White capture the pure essence of true friendship and help us understand how to be friends in the midst of these days."

—D. G. ELMORE, chairman, Elmore Companies Inc.; vice chairman, The Navigators

"Friendship. Is it just an elusive butterfly? Is its beauty real, and can it be captured? Or is it a woeful ode to love not realized? Mary and Jerry White let us capture the wonder and the beauty of friendship — of being and having friends."

—ALICE CANLIS, Canlis Restaurant

D0776514

TO BE A FRIEND

Building Deep and Lasting Relationships

JERRY & MARY WHITE

Discipleship Inside Out®

NavPress is the publishing ministry of The Navigators, an international Christian organization and leader in personal spiritual development. NavPress is committed to helping people grow spiritually and enjoy lives of meaning and hope through personal and group resources that are biblically rooted, culturally relevant, and highly practical.

For a free catalog go to www.NavPress.com.

To:
Merlyn and Dottie
Roger and Joanne
John and Jeanne
Ruth
John and Nancy
Ed and Merrilee
Helene
Chris and Alice
Stan and Lois
Doug and Kaylinn
Mike and Anne
Kim and Kari Ann
David and Lori
Dave and Myrna
Frank and Gloria
Scott and Kristi
Bill and Kathleen
Lee and Kelly
Paul and Phyllis
Donald and Jeanie
Jim and Marge
Mike and Chris
Terry and Carol

Friends of many years and many seasons who,
along with many others,
have immeasurably enriched our lives.

CONTENTS

PREFACE

GET A LIFE. Get a friend. But how? And why? If you picked up this book, you most likely have an interest in starting, developing, or repairing a relationship. Perhaps you're eager to get more out of your friendships, frustrated with current friends, or feeling lonely. Whatever your situation, this book can help you develop new friendships and enhance the ones you have.

To Be a Friend looks at friendship like a many-sided diamond, reflecting people's needs and aspirations. Most of us see friends through the lenses of our past relationships, both positive and negative experiences, and the desires of our hearts to know and be known. Friendship can be rewarding, fun, satisfying, and uplifting. It can also be confusing, frustrating, and disappointing. Which of these results depend on you? How much depends on the other person?

Expectations regarding friendship vary as much as people do, yet there are constants—basics—that flavor every relationship. In this book, we identify these basics to give you a framework for understanding your friendships in the past, present, and future. We want you to grasp the foundations of close friendships and recognize the problems and benefits of them. We also introduce the concept of virtuous friendship. Virtue gives a biblical and philosophical basis of friendship that goes beyond self-oriented relationships.

Much of the conscious development of our circle of friends rests on an understanding of the elements and concepts of friendship. In this book, we'll discuss:

- The foundation of good friendships
- The way to begin and develop friendships
- How to make and sustain lasting friendships
- How to repair broken or damaged friendships
- Networking your friendships

You won't find an automatic solution for making and keeping friends. Friendships take effort. They hold a bit of mystery. They can't be manufactured. Yet they are priceless. A friend can be one of the greatest spiritual and emotional treasures of our lives. When we lack true friends, we are isolated and lonely.

Walk with us as we probe and discover together the great adventure of being a friend and having friends.

Chapter 1

FRIENDS MATTER

Some people go to priests; others to poetry; I go to my friends.

VIRGINIA WOOLF

At the shrine of friendship never say die, let the wine of friendship never run dry.

VICTOR HUGO, LES MISÉRABLES

DO WE NEED FRIENDS? Most assuredly, yes! Friends are the lifeline to a fulfilling existence. They encourage us, counsel us, support us, rescue us, challenge us, and bring us joy. One of the saddest comments we heard when talking with people about their friendships was from a man who told us, "I had a friend once, but he died." Loneliness echoed in this plaintive statement as he described life without friends.

INDELIBLE FRIENDSHIP

Like steel threads, the bonds of friendship link us with people in our past and people in our present. They can even be stronger than family bonds. William Newton was a lanky boy from the deep south of Georgia who ended up in fighting in Iwo Jima during the bloody Pacific battles in World War II. He became fast friends with Roberts, a New Yorker. In the battle, they were side by side when William was twice wounded and evacuated. For fifty years, William assumed Roberts had been killed, and he still grieved for his friend. Then at a fifty-year reunion of veterans of Iwo Jima, he put his name on a sign-up page that later got into the hands of a retired New York police detective. Roberts immediately called William. William's son said, "Marines who had gone through the hell of war together and who each had been told that his best buddy had been killed in action were reunited. Then, and now, closer than brothers."[1]

As William and Roberts discovered, indelible connections of friendship are forged through childhood escapades, life transitions, selfless acts of kindness, and simply walking together through bonding experiences. Some of these friendships last; others fade until awakened by a memory or a chance reconnection.

We react differently with various friends; we also react differently when we're with just one friend rather than with a group. With a loud, boisterous friend, an introvert might try to be the same. If that introvert sits with another quiet friend, the tone and energy will be muted. Friendship dynamics differ markedly with each individual friend, in groups, in diverse contexts, and with our age and stage of life.

Each of our friends has contributed to the person we have become. We are a product of our families, our times, and our geographical roots. But friends mark us in profound ways. They alter our thinking, actions, desires, and ambitions, for good and for bad.

When we were young, our friendships grew in the soil of chance encounters, our parents' change of geography, our choice of college or university, and our early jobs. They were unplanned and unscripted, seemingly random. Yet, in reflection, God was present in each of them. Little did we know how these people would impact our lives. Each of our friends has contributed to the people we have become. We are a product of our families, our times, and our geographical roots. But friends mark us in profound ways. They alter our thinking, actions, desires, and ambitions, for good and for bad.

A LIFELINE TO A FULFILLING EXISTENCE

The need for friends spans all generations. Young children, teens, young adults, middle-aged adults, and seniors—all need friends. Friendships start in the family, where we learn acceptance, conflict resolution, enjoyment, and grace, or, on the negative side, rejection, conditional acceptance, and distrust. But a wide array of friendships outside of family enriches our lives in ways family can't. Friendships form the lifeblood of mental, emotional, and spiritual health.

Our need for trusted relationships runs deep. We long for someone who listens to us, understands us, and keeps confidences. When one of our daughters was in grade school, she would occasionally come home crying because a friend had abandoned her. We hugged her and told her we would always be there for her. No matter that a week later, she and her friend would be best friends again, our daughter's hurt was real. She missed her friend.

Psychiatrist Paul Tournier observed, "It is impossible to overemphasize the immense need humans have to be really listened to, to be taken seriously, to be understood."[2] Friends do these things for one another. Professionals such as pastors, psychologists, and counselors attempt to fill the void when friends do not. A friend of ours who is in counseling told us, "Really, my counselor just listens while I talk." Our friend is being helped because he feels heard and understood by this counselor.

A dear friend in his eighties reflected on his discovery of the need for friends. He said, "When I came home after college graduation, I was miserable. Why? Because I didn't have any friends to share life with. The depression into which I sank became so deep that it profoundly affected me the next two years. I was lonely beyond belief, even suicidal. I walked the streets at night, wishing I were dead. Decades were to pass before I was finally able to put all this into perspective and, at last, behind me." He concluded, "I've become convinced that I don't know a whole lot about friendship but also that I need it, I want it, and, surprise, it's a two-way street!"

We talked with a group of young twentysomethings about friendship, and one young man described the value of friendships this way: "I need friends in real-time experience. A friend is someone who will drop whatever he is doing in order to help me out if I need him. A close friend is someone I know I can count on." He continued, "Trust is key to close friendship. When I put my trust in someone, I believe that person is not going to turn around and use what I tell him in order to hurt me."

Some of our deepest experiences in friendship have come in relating for about three decades with three other couples in what we call our covenant group. In response to the question of why the eight of us are together, one woman said, "I think originally it was that we wanted to finish well. What makes it work? It's been iron sharpening iron, mental stimulation, discussing hard topics with one another, such as a child's death, cancer, and parents' deaths. So it's been life experiences. We've gone on trips together, spending lots of time with people we enjoy being with. Some have spent more time with others in the group and nobody cares. There's no jealousy or competition. We all know that when we leave, we'll all be better for having been together."

One man, emphasizing that these were not exclusive friendships, said, "I think if we all didn't need other friends, if we didn't have lots of friends, I don't think we would have stuck together, because when you're with people who feel they need you all the time, that's not friendship. I think we have rich friendship with each other and with many others."

This journey of friendship is not a superhighway. It leads us through the back roads of our lives and helps us see the scenery we miss if we go too fast.

> Lean on me when you're not strong
> And I'll be your friend; I'll help you carry on
> For it won't be long
> 'Til I'm gonna need somebody to lean on
>
> — BILL WITHERS

THOUGHTS and DISCUSSION

1. In what way do friends matter to you?
2. Discuss the kinds of friends you enjoy being with.
3. Look back on your early friendships. How did they evolve?

Chapter 2

MAKING FRIENDS

Friendship is like a flower. Water it, feed it, and wait for the
sun and soil to make it grow.

UNKNOWN

In everyone's life, at some time, our inner fire goes out.
It's then burst into flame by an encounter by another
human being. We should all be grateful for those people
who rekindle the inner spirit.

ALBERT SCHWEITZER

THE TWO OF US met at the University of Washington during
our sophomore year. Mary wanted to attend a local church on
Sunday and called the church office for directions to get there on
the city bus. She was told it was a complicated and lengthy ride with
three bus changes. But there was an alternative. Some students from
the university attended the church and drove there every Sunday.
She was given a few names and phone numbers. She called one:
Jerry White. The next Sunday, Jerry drove to Mary's dorm and
appeared in the lobby. There was no instant attraction, just one stu-
dent meeting another.

But over the next several months, the acquaintance changed to a growing friendship. Mary admired Jerry's leadership qualities, his genuine friendships, and his intellect. He liked Mary's flaming-red hair, her quiet demeanor, and her spiritually sensitive family. As the rides to and from the church continued along with other opportunities to see one another on campus, the friendship deepened. Jerry would appear in the quad, a grouping of buildings that formed the original campus, and meet Mary after class. Occasionally she would skip geology to spend time with Jerry. Her grade in that class was the lowest grade of her university career, but the rewards of spending time with Jerry rather than taking notes in geology class have been lifelong. Mary would much rather spend life with him than with stones and rocks of every variety!

Just as our friendship had a beginning point, so does every friendship. Eyes meet. Hands clasp. Gracious words are exchanged. No one knows where an introduction will go. Most go nowhere. Rarely do we identify someone and think, *I will set out to be his friend*. Brief meetings are just that: momentary encounters. They are casual, short-lived, and pleasant, but over soon. In fortunate cases, the strangers linger, talk longer, and realize common interests and attraction. A few of these encounters may grow into casual friendships or even lifelong relationships.

That was the case for Mary and her friend Lyla. They met when Mary was six and Lyla was four. Their parents attended the same church. Throughout their school days, they were the best of friends. When Mary left for college, the friendship continued, especially because Mary's brother had the good sense to marry Lyla. Mary and Lyla have remained friends for a lifetime, connected by family and a loving camaraderie. They have weathered some difficult events together, and the friendship has required effort on both their parts. They talk often as friends and are committed to each other far beyond their family ties. Although they live geographically far apart, their friendship remains strong.

Close friendships do not just happen. In many ways, they are like a garden. Gardeners sow seeds, water, fertilize, and prune if they want to grow delicious vegetables. But there is much that gardeners cannot control: the amount of sunshine, whether the seeds are good or bad, and the amount of rainfall.

Colorado is a tough climate in which to have a garden, but we try. Mary works at it. Jerry observes! Some gardeners, like Jerry, possess little or no intuition or skill for that task. Several years ago, Mary left for a brief trip a few days after Christmas. The decorations remained in place during her absence. When she returned, Jerry proudly announced that every night, he had brought the poinsettias in from the front porch, concerned they would freeze. Mary told him as kindly as she could that she appreciated his thoughtfulness but that the flowers were artificial!

Similar to growing gardens, if we want friends, we must plant a certain kind of seeds and nurture them with attention, skill, persistence, and time. Then we must wait to see if friendships grow.

Wishing to be friends is quick work, but friendship is a slow ripening fruit. — *Aristotle*

You say, "That's a nice analogy, but I need some direction and guidance." So let's walk down that path.

FACTORS IN FRIENDSHIP FORMATION

The two of us spent our childhoods in small towns in the Midwest. Jerry grew up in a tiny town of a hundred people. He likes to tell people that his phone number was 9, which indicated both the size of the town and his age. The friends he made there have lasted a lifetime, and he is warmly welcomed whenever he returns. Mary grew up on a farm near a town of five hundred people. Society was stable and constant in those towns. Friendship pools were limited but faithful and lasted through old age. For people living in small communities today, the same is still true. But "back then" has disappeared, and we're in a different environment.

Times have changed. Today most people live in urban environments and move frequently. We no longer enjoy years of daily contact with friends we met in elementary school. People come and go in our lives, usually due to changing circumstances or interests.

As we meet people, what then gives us stimulus to develop a friendship? What factors need to be present in order for a friendship to grow?

Mutual Attraction

Have you ever met someone and felt that something clicked in that encounter? Maybe you walked away thinking, *I would really like to know that person better.* Perhaps it's an attraction to personality, intellect, similar interests, or a common background. Similar backgrounds, education, occupations, or experiences make the possibility of a friendship more inviting. Mentally or emotionally, you are drawn to the possibility of connecting again.

When Jerry discovers that someone is a fellow handball player or has served in the Air Force, he experiences an immediate connection with that person. It might be just a surface connection, but it opens the door to the possibility of a more significant relationship.

There are exceptions, of course. Not every relationship is based on common interests. In her book *An Invisible Thread*,[1] Laura Schroff, a Caucasian, middle-aged woman, befriends an eleven-year-old African-American boy on the streets of New York. Contrary to her custom of bypassing panhandlers, she pauses, engages in conversation with a hungry little boy, and buys him a meal. Thus begins a lifelong friendship of two very disparate people.

Circumstances

In the course of our lives, circumstances throw us together with certain people. In a cluster of eight houses at the United States Air Force Academy, where we lived for four years, every family had young children—twenty-six of them on our cul-de-sac. Our families were drawn together by our common circumstances and location. On warm summer nights, the children would play outdoor games until dark while the parents visited. We shared babysitting and carpooling. We went to football games. We ate in each other's homes. We depended on each other in emergencies.

Here's a case in point. One summer evening, we called one of our daughters, Kathy, in for dinner, but she decided to take one more spin around the block on her bicycle. In her haste to get back to the dinner table, she rounded a corner too sharply, steered off the sidewalk, flew across the hood of an oncoming car, and landed in the street. Hearing yelling outdoors, we hurried and saw our daughter lying motionless on the pavement. Friends jumped in to take care of our other kids so we could rush our daughter to the hospital. When we know we can depend on someone to be there for us, it nurtures a friendship with that person. Fortunately, Kathy suffered only a minor concussion and some painful scrapes, but the driver of the car was understandably shocked and never did become a good friend!

We also click with people whose life circumstances are similar to ours: going through cancer treatment, parenting children with learning disabilities, being a single mom, working in the same profession, going through a divorce, or losing a job. Many relationships emerge from groups such as Bible Study Fellowship, Community Bible Studies, The Navigators, Cru, InterVarsity, or some other group connection. In church, friendships result when people are together in small groups or special-interest support groups.

In the summer of 2012, the Waldo Canyon Fire destroyed almost 350 homes and killed two people near our neighborhood in Colorado Springs. This tragedy brought many people together in rebuilding a community and supporting one another. We were forced to evacuate with thousands of others as the fire raged. When we were allowed to return home days later, neighbors, some of whom we had never met, stood in the street sharing stories and forging new relationships. Common circumstances present opportunities for friendships to begin and be nurtured.

Intentionality

For a friendship to form, someone has to take the initiative. We invite people into our couples' Bible study with the hope that it will be a seedbed for friendships. We invite people to our home for a meal or accept someone else's invitation. We join or sponsor a neighborhood barbecue. In order to have a presence for Christ and for a friendship to form, we must simply show up.

We met our longtime friends Chris and Alice through a mutual friend who suggested that Chris meet Jerry. The two of them met in a restaurant near the Seattle-Tacoma airport. After a couple hours of talking, they realized that the two of them could be friends, so they decided to see if their wives would enjoy each other as well. Jerry spontaneously invited Chris and his family to come over for dinner the next night. When Mary found out that Chris and Alice owned a famous five-star restaurant, she felt a bit intimidated, and it set off a round of "discussions" with Jerry. Even so, Chris and Alice came to our house for dinner. The menu has long been forgotten, but the friendship that began that night has lasted for decades.

No friendship is a one-way street. Even when someone takes initiative, the other person must respond.

The old saying "It takes two to tango" holds true in friendship. No friendship is a one-way street. Even when someone takes initiative, the other person must respond. Perhaps one person wants the relationship, but the other shows no interest. Maybe one person has a full friendship circle and cannot add more or there is simply no appeal or attraction that leads to further contact. That's fine: Better no friendship than a forced one.

We often attend Air Force and business social events in Colorado Springs. At times when we're tired or busy, we attend out of obligation. Usually, though, we pray, *Lord, who do you want us to meet and talk to at this event?* Again and again, our intentional openness has led to the beginnings of a relationship or an open door to friendship and spiritual influence.

Some of you may be thinking, *The last thing I need is another relationship!* This may be true, especially for introverts. However, and this is a big "however," it is important to keep the door open for the relationships God wants us to have. We may be delightfully surprised by the people He brings our way.

This has happened for us many times over the years. One December afternoon, we drove to a Christmas reception at Petersen Air Force Base in Colorado Springs. We went through the commander's receiving line, stayed for a short while, and prepared to leave. As we were walking out, Jerry glanced back and said, "I need to greet Bob." In that short encounter, Bob told Jerry he needed to serve with the Air Force Association's Aerospace Education Foundation. That led to a decade of Jerry's involvement with the Air Force Association and many renewed and new friendships.

Another time, Jerry was in Chico, California, to speak at a men's luncheon for his friend Dwight. He told Jerry he needed to meet a man he was helping in his walk with God. Dwight thought there would be common interests. He said, "He has a PhD." Jerry, who also has a PhD, envisioned a stuffy, perhaps dull, academic. What a surprise! Doug was, and is, a vibrant, thoughtful, astute businessman and follower of Jesus. As Jerry heard his story, he said, "I have a friend you really need to meet. His name is Chris." Jerry arranged a meeting between Doug and Chris a couple of months later. The two have been close friends ever since. Doug and Chris consistently encourage one another in their businesses and spiritual lives. Both men are part of our covenant group.

Time and Opportunity

We should not expect instant friendship. Friendships grow over years, not months, often through repeated and consistent contact. As a friendship is developing, each person, perhaps unknowingly, is testing the waters. Getting involved in activities and organizations such as the PTA, church, a child's athletic event, or a civic organization can broaden our connections and allow room for friendships to grow.

Younger people are often adept at broadening their connections. They love to run in a group, gather in homes, meet in pubs, and plan hikes together. This carries into their early years of marriage, where the mutual interests of babies, new careers, and new experiences draw them together. As we get older, we tend to get busier and less involved in spontaneous activities.

Testing

Although this is not a factor in initiating friendships, it is a vital factor as the friendship progresses, as no friendship develops beyond a casual state without some testing. This comes in the form of mutual disagreements, arguments, misunderstandings, offenses, conflicts, and feelings of tension. Sometimes the testing is more outward and verbal. Sometimes it is inward and just sensed. The ability to disagree and remain friends deepens the relationship; the inability to disagree with each other often causes a break. We cannot think of a friendship of ours in which there has not been some level of tension or conflict.

Common Interests

Work, church, parents' associations, children's sports activities, school events, and charity events and efforts often bring people of common interests together. Garden clubs, skeet shooting, hunting and fishing clubs, political clubs, book clubs, alumni associations, and sports teams all provide opportunities for relationships to develop. When we connect while "doing" something, we see people in a different light than we do when we meet them for a cup of coffee, at a party, or in a brief encounter. At work, we get assigned to a project team. In church, we join a committee. In the neighborhood, we start a clothing drive for the homeless. Each opens the possibility of new friendships.

Friendships without some level of common interest in work, family, or hobbies seldom develop into lasting relationships. When we have an overlapping interest that draws us together, we are more likely to enjoy being together—a necessary element of friendship. Many of our relationships evolved from our Navigator discipleship contacts, our Air Force community, and school activities with our children.

Mike and Anne came into our lives when Mike and Jerry worked together in the Air Force and also played handball together. That led to our involvement in a Bible study, traveling together, and a significant friendship. One bonding experience took place when we traveled together in Europe in a rental car. We took a wrong turn and found ourselves straddling some railroad tracks. Down the line, we saw the light of an approaching train. After some hasty maneuvering, we drove off the tracks and stopped the car to let our heartbeats slow down. Bonding!

Mutual Openness and Transparency

Friendships do not develop or deepen with casual chitchat. Both close and intimate friendships grow as we begin to open our minds and hearts to one another, discussing matters of substance. Certainly we all talk about surfaces issues, such as schedules, kids, current events, and generalities. These conversations form the groundwork for deeper interactions about specific needs regarding children, family, our health, spiritual needs, and hurts and joys. But for that to happen, someone must open up and be vulnerable. Friendships are built on degrees of openness. One of the first signs of a deepening friendship is when one person shares a problem or need in his or her life.

We should not spill our guts in every conversation. The wise person puts out "feelers" such as the following to see what he or she can reveal beyond the surface:

- "One of our kids is struggling in school."
- "No one told me marriage would be this hard."
- "It's a tough day at work."
- "The doc told me there's something suspicious on the CAT scan."
- "My husband never prays with me."

These throw-away comments are a probe for seeing if the other person wants to go deeper. Our friend Jean sent out feelers to see if people at church wanted to go beyond the casual greetings following the service. As she met people in the church corridor, she would ask them, "How are you really doing?" After a month, she stopped asking. So many people responded truthfully and asked for additional time with her that she had to relate to those friends before adding more.

There is a risk to being transparent. Sometimes doing so opens the door to hurt and misunderstanding. Mary once told a friend that one of our children was struggling over something and asked for prayer. Before the friend prayed, she said, "We must be doing something right because all of our children are doing fine." That offhand comment, probably not intended to hurt, did so deeply.

PRACTICAL SUGGESTIONS FOR MAKING FRIENDS

Will your friendships grow? Many will, some won't, but you will grow as you extend yourself to others. Plant the seed and take care of that garden. Here are some practical suggestions for how to do that:

- **Be there.** The simplicity of presence opens many doors—for friendship, influence, connections, and pleasure.
- **Make an effort.** Take initiative in connecting with people.
- **Hold friendships in an open hand.** No one wants to be obligated to pursue a friendship. Friendships do not have strings attached. Possessiveness should not be part of friendship. No one owns another's friendship.

JESUS IN THE MIDDLE OF EVERY RELATIONSHIP

A last but extremely important thought as you grow friendships: If you are a believer, Jesus needs to be in the middle of each of your relationships. Your faith defines who you are. Your relationship with Jesus allows you to give and love unconditionally.

If friendship is devoid of any discussion of life in Christ and the spiritual dimension, it will never grow to full maturity. We have known friendships where both were believers but rarely, if ever, discussed the deeper issues of faith. Without spiritual stimulation, a friendship cannot grow in depth.

Although believers can certainly have friends who do not have a relationship with Jesus, we need to make sure He is part of our interactions. It is not necessary for every conversation to be a spiritual one. Spiritual matters should simply be part of the ebb and flow of relating. When two friends know where the other is coming from spiritually, it becomes the underlying soil in which the friendship grows. A friendship that hides or ignores our most foundational life relationship does not bear the stamp of authenticity. When we deepen our personal walk with Jesus, our capacity and ability to be a friend increases immeasurably.

THOUGHTS and DISCUSSION

1. Describe how one or two of your closest friendships began.
2. Do you find it more difficult or easier to make friendships now than years ago? Why do you think that is the case?
3. What have been the major mutual attractions in your friendships?
4. What have been the major factors in whether your friendships have grown?
5. How prevalent is spiritual conversation in your friendships? Does it really matter? Explain your answer.

Chapter 3

THE LEGO FACTOR: BUILDING CLOSE FRIENDSHIPS

If you have built castles in the air, your work need not be lost. That is where they should be. Now put the foundations under them.

HENRY DAVID THOREAU

Friendship is unnecessary, like philosophy, like art. . . . It has no survival value. Rather, it is one of those things that give value to survival.

C. S. LEWIS

OUR GRANDSON JOSH LOVED Legos as he was growing up. Every Christmas or birthday we knew what to buy him as a gift: more Legos. If he had the right parts, he could build anything — cars, spaceships, airplanes, trucks, bridges, buildings. Sometimes he had a guide or a pattern. Other times, he would simply start and see what developed. For each project, Josh had a plan, a foundation, a picture in his mind of the end result. We watched the process as he built: trying, undoing some sections, retrying until a finished structure emerged. Some designs didn't work or fell apart or looked strange. Occasionally he added more Legos to make the structure better. Trial and error and patience made the building process work.

All human relationships grow in a similar fashion. We begin, try to build, try again, look for a response, and see what develops.

WHAT IS A CLOSE FRIEND?

It's been said, "If you aim at nothing, you're sure to hit it." Most of us have a picture in our minds of what a friend should be. It's most likely an emotional picture rather than the result of a studied definition. In the course of our research for writing this book, we asked various people to tell us how they defined a close friend. The following comments are representative of the answers we received:

- "Someone you can bare your soul to and not be afraid it will get around. Someone who shares loving concern and tactful truth." (woman, age 31)
- "One who knows you well and loves you anyway." (woman, age 66)
- "Loyal in hard times, fun to be with, and has common interests." (man, age 26)
- "A person who understands you, appreciates your views, loyal. A person who has quite a few interests in common with you." (man, age 52)
- "Someone who knows me intimately and is committed to my best under all circumstances, regardless of the risks to our relationship." (man, age 31)

Individual experiences differ, and each of these responses is a subjective *perception* of friendship. But certain phrases and words appear repeatedly in the responses, revealing what most people want in a close friendship: loyalty, sharing, confidentiality, and mutual interests.

One difficulty in describing a friend is that not all friends are the same. We have work friends, neighborhood friends, childhood friends, college friends, relatives, family friends, and friends from among our children's parents. We think of them differently and relate to them in different ways. Nor do people have the same definition of what a friend is. In a phone call, Jerry may tell someone, "Bill is a close friend." After the call, Mary will say, "A close friend? But you just met him a month ago!" This disparity is normal. People are either restrictive or expansive in their idea of friendship.

We would like to help you think constructively about yourself, your thoughts, and your experiences with friends and give you a framework for understanding the different types of friends you have. To make the most of this process, you will need a desire to develop new friendships and make the friendships you have better by improving your relating skills.

THE CIRCLES OF FRIENDSHIP

Life is built around many different kinds of friendships. We often distinguish our friends by such terms as new friend, close friend, good friend, real friend, and more. It has been helpful for us to view our various kinds of friendships as four overlapping circles:

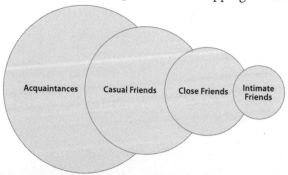

Keep in mind that although this illustration reflects the intertwining of friendships, it does not fully reflect reality. No illustration can. Friendships and people are complex. Friends flow back and forth between these circles, and we can't pigeonhole people into one circle or another.

Now let's take a closer look at each of these four types of friends.

Acquaintances

Every friend, including our spouse, was once an acquaintance. Have you ever wondered about God's place in all of these encounters? Did the two of us just "happen" to meet at the University of Washington? We don't think so. We believe that God leads people into their connections and conversations. Under God's leadership, life is not random. It may at times seem random, but it is not.

As we look back over our many friendships, we are intrigued at how they began. We met two of our lifelong friends at a chapel service at Patrick Air Force Base. We invited this couple to a small Bible study in our home the following week. They were fairly new in their life as believers, so they wondered what they were getting themselves into. All that week they debated about whether to accept our invitation. They came, and that began a life of intersecting careers, families, and friendship.

People make acquaintances everywhere: at grocery store checkouts, restaurants, parties, work, sports events, school functions. These friendships are unplanned and the interactions brief. We estimate that a person makes between five hundred and fifteen hundred acquaintances a year. Only a few of these will develop beyond that initial contact. Most will simply remain acquaintances whom we occasionally greet. But on occasion, something sparks, prompting more interaction and moving the person into the next circle.

Casual Friends

Many of us maintain a large number of casual friends. We greet them by their first name but may not even know their last name. We see them regularly at work, the athletic club, or church. We stop and chat, each time learning a little more about them. We might not do anything social or intentional with them. Depending on how outgoing we are, we can have dozens to hundreds of casual friends.

Casual friends are the "oil in the gears" of living; they form the "stuff" of which our community is made: at the bank, grocery store, workplace, church. When a grocery clerk says, "Hi, Mrs. White," Mary feels the comfort of being in familiar territory and of being recognized. Casual friendships set a tone in our life interactions and open the possibility for future friendships.

Jerry has a locker at our local YMCA on a particular row. So does "Coach." The two of them pass the time of day with little substance in the midst of chatter from others. Roger, too, works out at the Y. He and Jerry share an Air Force background. They chat and banter, but the conversation goes no deeper. Both of these friendships will remain casual until some event or need takes the friendship to another level. The number of casual friends a person has depends on one's personality, context, age, and stage of life.

Close Friends

This circle contains most of the meaningful relationships we experience. Close friends encourage and inspire us. While some people are happy with only a few close friends, some people can maintain twenty to thirty at a given time. This number is variable depending on your personality type: extrovert or introvert. There is no special merit badge for having a huge number of close friends; it is the quality and context of those friendships that matter.

Close friendships develop as we have repeated contact with one another. We see some close friends in our home or in theirs. We see others while engaged in mutual activities. Contact isn't the only factor in forming close friendships. There must be sharing on a deeper level, getting to know the thoughts and feelings of our close friends. Because ours is a mobile society, many close friends live in other cities or states. They connect regularly through phone calls or some form of social media.

There are many levels even inside this category of close friends. For instance, we have friends at work, friends within the family, and personal friends. We also have people we consider our mentors, or people whom we mentor. Often our mentors and mentees are at a different age or stage of life. Then we have friends we just know and like to be with. In this circle of close friends, we have some who are closer than others, but all are close.

This is a dynamic, diverse, and fluid category. Close friends bring support, joy, caring, encouragement, and motivation into our lives, regardless of the environment in which we meet them.

Intimate (Best) Friends

These friends are rare and few in number. They are the people we trust most deeply, share with most intimately, and depend on most strongly. They bring zest to our lives, and we cherish them for a lifetime. We estimate that most people will have only three to five best friends over a lifetime. This is not a rule, just an observation. Rudyard Kipling wrote a wonderful poem about friendship, "A Thousandth Man."

One man in a thousand, Solomon says,
Will stick more close than a brother.
And it's worth seeking him half your days
If you find him before the other.
Nine hundred and ninety-nine depend
On what the world sees in you,
But the Thousandth Man will stand your friend
With the whole round world agin you.[1]

We should not become discouraged or impatient at the high bar of such a friendship. It is an ideal. Intimate friendships grow and develop over time. Be patient.

While personality and experience play a part in the breadth and depth of our friendships, we assert this principle: Every person has the capacity to develop intimate friendships. Let's take a look at the factors that cause a casual friendship to deepen into a close or even intimate friendship.

BUILDING STRONG AND INTIMATE FRIENDSHIPS

Our house in Colorado Springs is built in an area with bentonite clay in the earth. Rain causes the clay to expand, and if the clay is near the foundation of the house, the clay, like a huge vise, will crush the foundation. To prevent this from happening, the contractor has to dig a trench about twenty feet below and on the sides of the foundation and then refill it with soil and sand that does not expand. A proper foundation prevents future disasters. Poor foundations can be repaired, but at great cost. Friendships, too, can benefit from having a strong foundation.

As we talked with people about how they built strong friendships, as many as twenty ideas were mentioned. Most were interrelated and overlapping, but a few essential characteristics emerged. Please note that every friendship reflects all these characteristics in varying degrees of depth. However, an intimate friendship reflects almost all of these to a large degree.

Here are five critical building blocks that comprise the foundation for a strong and intimate friendship. Are they exhaustive? Probably not. These five contain many other subsets of ideas.

1. Trust

Most of the people we interviewed said that trust and confidentiality were of significant importance to having a close friendship.

Few delights can equal the presence of one whom we trust utterly. — George MacDonald

What is trust? It is knowing that any and all communication is safe with a friend. Confidentiality is a given; we are certain our friend will not break our confidence. Trust builds slowly over time. We watch and test others to be sure they are trustworthy. While discussing arms control with President Mikhail Gorbachev, President Ronald Reagan quoted a Russian proverb, saying, "Trust, but verify." Knowingly, or unknowingly, we all instinctively practice this proverb. We want to make sure we can trust someone in small matters. If we can, then we entrust that person with deeper things. When trust is broken, relationships begin to shatter.

A blessed thing it is for any man or woman to have a friend, one human soul whom we can trust utterly, who knows the best and worst of us and who loves us in spite of all our faults. — Charles Kingsley

2. Stimulation

Some people stimulate your mind, energize your imagination, and stir your soul. They might not always make you comfortable, but they do help you grow and become a better person. Other people seem boring, at least to you, because you do not connect with them emotionally, intellectually, or spiritually.

Those we associate with determine much of what we do, think, and believe. Our friendships cause us to change, for good or bad. For this reason, many of our friendships should push us to walk with Jesus more deeply. The apostle Paul wrote, "Let us consider how to stimulate one another to love and good deeds" (Hebrews 10:24, NASB), and Peter said, "I have tried to stimulate your wholesome thinking and refresh your memory" (2 Peter 3:1, NLT). Proverbs says, "He who walks with wise men will be wise, but the companion of fools will suffer harm" (13:20, NASB). This verse challenges our choice of relationships. *The Message* states it more bluntly: "Hang out with fools and watch your life fall to pieces."

Intellectual stimulation is also important. We need people in our lives who make us think, who challenge us and push us to new ways of living. In the 1930s, a group of men in Oxford, England, called themselves "The Inklings." C. S. Lewis, J. R. R. Tolkien, Charles Williams, and several others met to discuss their writings. It was more than a group of academics spinning intellectual webs. They criticized and inspired each other's thinking. We have similar kinds of interaction with the people in our covenant group. We meet together for three days semiannually and always choose a topic or book to discuss together. We laugh, argue, question, and grow.

Jerry has a friend, who, in any discussion will ask, "Now, why is that?" The question promotes good thinking. Intellectual stimulation goes beyond high sounding or esoteric discussions. It forces us to think in new ways.

3. Fun

Fun seasons a friendship with laughter and pleasure. Fun gives relief to solemn, heavy discussions and brings friends together in special ways. (See chapter 12, "Let's Party!" for details on fun in friendship.)

4. Love

No friendship can be at an intimate level without love. The Bible describes more than one kind of love. *Agape love* displays the pure, accepting, grace-filled, enveloping love that God shows us. We try to emulate it but all fall short. Most of us experience and offer *phileo love* (brotherly love). Certainly, *phileo* love is legitimate and sustains our friendships, but we always want to be moving toward *agape* love, as expressed in 1 Corinthians 13:4-7:

> Love is very patient and kind, never jealous or envious, never boastful or proud, never haughty or selfish or rude. Love does not demand its own way. It is not irritable or touchy. It does not hold grudges and will hardly even notice when others do it wrong. It is never glad about injustice, but rejoices whenever truth wins out. If you love someone, you will be loyal to him no matter what the cost. You will always believe in him, always expect the best of him, and always stand your ground in defending him. (TLB)

Friends long for—even demand—that kind of love. Years ago, Mary decided to remove wallpaper and give the front entrance of our home a new look. From a high perch on a shaky stepladder, she reached too far and tumbled twelve feet to the concrete floor, striking a handrail on the way down and breaking six ribs. Jerry was attending meetings in another part of the country. When our friend Alice heard the news, she arranged for professionals to finish removing the wallpaper and paint the wall. She brought food and flowers to the house. Mary remembers that loving act to this day.

In Jesus' final conversation with Peter, He asked him two times, "Do you love [*agape*] me?" Peter's answer, "I am fond [*phileo*] of you" (see John 21:15-17). The third time Jesus asked Peter if he loves Him, Jesus used the word *phileo* instead of *agape*. He was accommodating Peter. We as mortals can love in a deeper way but find it difficult to go beyond *phileo* to *agape*. We need to unashamedly build *agape* love into our deepest friendships. *Agape* love leads to a kind of love that is self-sacrificing and virtuous.

5. Self-Sacrifice

This concept finds expression in many sacred and secular writings. We honor people who sacrifice their life for others. We know that

Jesus' love for us ended in His dying for us: "Love each other as I have loved you. Greater love has no one than this: to lay down one's life for one's friends" (John 15:12-13). Self-sacrifice is so important in friendship that we devote an entire chapter ("How Much Does Friendship Cost?") to this idea. There are other characteristics of friendship that are important, such as loyalty and deep sharing. You will see them emerge as we describe aspects of friendship.

So consider the building blocks of close friendship and how they form the foundations upon which great friendships are built. Remember, how you build in the early stages of a friendship will determine the health and longevity of that friendship.

THOUGHTS and DISCUSSION

1. Discuss the validity of the Circles of Friendship concept.
2. Estimate the number of friends you have in each circle.
3. Write out your definition of a friend.
4. Which of the building blocks is easiest for you to do? Which is most difficult? Explain your answer.

Chapter 4

VIRTUOUS FRIENDSHIP

What is a friend? A single soul dwelling in two bodies.

ARISTOTLE

The superior man thinks always of virtue; the common man thinks of comfort.

CONFUCIUS

Only God can give us a selfless love for others, as the Holy Spirit changes us from within.

BILLY GRAHAM

WALT, AN AIR FORCE colonel, was Jerry's mentor in the early days of the space program at Cape Canaveral. Jerry left Cape Canaveral to study for a master's degree, and when Walt heard that Jerry was about to accept an assignment to teach at the United States Air Force Academy, he called and pleaded with Jerry to reject the assignment. He wanted to intercede and find what he felt would be a better career-enhancing assignment. He didn't have to do that. He simply cared for Jerry as his friend and mentor. Jerry did not take his offer, as he felt that God clearly wanted us at the Academy, but we have remembered Walt's kindness and concern.

The same for Bill and Doris. When we were young marrieds, they brought us into their home and included us in a Bible study at Webb Air Force Base in Big Spring, Texas. They loved us, taught us, and walked with us through a major career change. Bill and Doris became lifelong friends, though we saw them infrequently because of changing assignments in the Air Force. Their friendship influenced our parenting, strengthened our faith, and counseled our future in the military.

These were virtuous friendships.

Most of us are unknowingly selfish when it comes to friendship. We ask ourselves, *How will this benefit me? What do I get out of it? Does this friendship make me feel good?* Yet if a friendship is for only our own benefit, it will not last. In this chapter, we want to examine the qualities that make a virtuous friendship.

DESCRIBING VIRTUOUS FRIENDSHIP

In *The Book of Virtues*, Bill Bennett told collected stories that illustrate the great historic virtues of self-discipline, compassion, responsibility, friendship, work, courage, perseverance, honesty, loyalty, and faith. Each of these expresses itself to some degree in virtuous friendships.[1]

To understand virtuous friendship, we first need to define *virtue*. The *Merriam-Webster's* dictionary defines it as: (a) conforming to a standard of right: morality (b) a particular moral excellence. *Learner's* dictionary says: (a) morally good behavior or character. Virtue has a solid, moral base. It goes beyond self-interest and looks to what is right and good for others, including individuals, communities, and nations.

The word *virtue* is used many times in the Bible. Verses 10 and 29 of Proverbs 31 call the ideal wife a woman of virtue: "Who can find a virtuous woman? for her price is far above rubies. . . . Many daughters have done virtuously, but thou excellest them all" (KJV). Other translations use the words *good*, *fine*, and *noble*, all descriptive of virtue. Regarding Ruth, Boaz said, "All the people of my town know that you are a virtuous woman" (Ruth 3:11, NKJV). Boaz wasn't speaking of Ruth's sexual morality; he was saying that she conducted herself in such a way that everyone knew she was upright, loyal, and obedient to the law. Even though she was a foreigner, she was respected. Her selfless and energetic care for her mother-in-law impressed the local villagers. Her selfless actions toward her "kinsman redeemer" and future husband made her virtuous. She conducted herself with honor in the eyes of the community.

Virtue has a solid, moral base. It goes beyond self-interest and looks to what is right and good for others, including individuals, communities, and nations.

In the Greek New Testament, the word *arepe*, which is translated *virtue* in English, means "goodness, strength and moral courage."[2] Peter lists *virtue* as one of the character traits to be emulated and growing in one's life.

> Make every effort to add to your faith goodness [virtue]; and to goodness [virtue], knowledge; and to knowledge, self-control; and to self-control, perseverance; and to perseverance, godliness; and to godliness, mutual affection; and to mutual affection, love. (2 Peter 1:5-7)

Virtue, brotherly kindness, and love contribute to virtuous friendship. Virtue is bigger, broader, deeper, and more meaningful than can be summarized by a dictionary. Is it character? Yes. Can nonbelievers have virtue? Most certainly. Many of the founders of the United States were deists. They believed the moral teachings of Jesus, but not necessarily that Jesus was Lord and Savior. Yet they saw that the behavior of leaders should reflect the teachings of Jesus and the Bible — that is, be virtuous, for the good of others, to protect the dignity of every citizen, to guard their rights, to honor their value to God. They resolved to establish a nation of virtuous people under the care and direction of virtuous leaders who would put the good of the nation before their own personal interests. Even in the heat of political battle and disagreement, they formed deep friendships reflecting virtue. One of the most notable was the friendship between John Adams, a committed believer, and Thomas Jefferson, a deist. Although they were on opposite sides of the political spectrum, the two men corresponded extensively as friends. Interestingly, these heroes of the American story died on the same day: July 4, 1826.

History records many people who acted selflessly. Martin Luther King Jr. spoke boldly for his fellow African-Americans, putting his life at risk. George Washington declined a third term as president when he could have been made king. He acted selflessly, knowing that the nation fought to escape a monarchy, not to establish one. Dawson Trotman, founder of The Navigators, died while rescuing a drowning girl. He died as he lived, always holding someone up. Countless numbers of unknown people daily serve the homeless, care for orphans, give free medical service, and dig wells in underdeveloped countries, serving with no acclaim, credit, or expectation of receiving anything in return.

The concept of virtuous friendship goes back to Aristotle. He proposed three kinds of friendship. The first was for utilitarian purposes — that which is beneficial to you in terms of connections, money, prestige, and so on. A friendship like this takes much and gives little. The second kind was for pleasure. Again, this kind of friendship is mostly self-serving, or based on "what it gives me." According to Aristotle, the highest sense of friendship is to "do good toward a friend purely for the sake of the friend."[3] This is virtuous friendship. It seeks the other person's good in a manner that is selfless and self-sacrificing.

While virtue gives, expecting nothing in return, there is a return, though it is not the primary motivation for giving. Perhaps the best example of a virtuous relationship is a mother or father with their baby son or daughter. Parents give, serve, sacrifice, and protect their children with no return of appreciation or recompense. Yet they receive great pleasure in giving, watching for those signs of growth and response. There is no thought that their children owe them. Then, as they mature, children begin to give back to their parents in many ways. Similarly, people often respond with deep appreciation to acts of virtue that come their way from others.

Ideally a virtuous person acts with virtue toward everyone. It can be argued that one cannot fully love another without loving oneself. This is the idea behind the Golden Rule. Jesus said, "Do to others as you would have them do to you" (Luke 6:31). When we appreciate and love who we are and who God made us to be, we can feel the same about our friends. It's a tall order to "do to others." Too often we're busy concentrating on our own needs and preferences and fail to see that our friends need the same thing we desire and need. Virtue looks beyond the surface and sees the God-created person within. This brings to mind such people as Charles Colson and Mother Teresa, who dedicated their lives to helping others: prisoners, the disenfranchised, the sickest of the sick, the poorest of the poor, and the dying.

Are we saying that every friendship must fit only this altruistic pattern? Definitely not. We are not robots. We are humans who thrive on giving and receiving love. But we do so imperfectly. Is there anything we do that does not have some aspect of self-serving? Even so, every relationship should have an element of virtue. We must treat every person we encounter with honor and respect, even though we might never meet that person again. If this sounds daunting, remember that as followers of Jesus, we have access to power far beyond ourselves. We draw upon the Holy Spirit and an inner motivation. The secret lies in recognizing and applying that power. We need a combination of biblical truth, wise counsel from others and their experiences, and willingness to learn and change. When virtuous friendship is played out among friends, each one is enriched beyond what he or she gives.

Every relationship should have an element of virtue.

DEVELOPING LONG-LASTING, VIRTUOUS FRIENDSHIPS

In discussing virtues, Bill Bennett said that these virtues do not come naturally to children but must be taught. So it is in friendship. We need to be taught what a virtuous friendship is. Bennett described the demands of friendship: "For frankness, for self-revelation, for taking friends' criticisms as seriously as their expressions of admiration or praise, for stand-by-me loyalty and for assistance to the point of self-sacrifice — are all potent encouragements to moral maturation and even enoblement."[4]

When we practice virtue, we lay the foundation for a lasting friendship. By "lasting friendships," we refer to those with both longevity and depth. These are not always intimate friendships. Most often they are close friends, sprinkled with some casual friends. All of us garner more and more friends as we move through life. Maintaining and nurturing relationships takes time and energy. We offer what we can to each relationship, including virtue.

For a relationship to grow into a long-lasting friendship, friends must share some bonding experiences. Dictionary.com has an interesting definition of *bonding*: "a close friendship that develops between adults, often as a result of intense experiences, as those shared in military combat." The New Testament frequently uses military or battle imagery. In the early church, persecution was a constant threat and reality. As the early believers worked together to evangelize, teach truth, and survive physically, they formed deep bonds. We see these illustrated in Romans 16, where Paul ended his incredibly doctrinal letter with surprisingly personal comments. He listed twenty-seven good friends in this one communication. He used the phrase *dear friend* three times. The Greek word is *agapeton* ("beloved, dearly beloved by me"). Consider the phrases he used to describe these close friends:

- Sister, servant of the church in Cenchreae (verse 1)
- A great help to me (verse 2)
- Fellow workers (verses 3,9)
- Risk their lives for me (verse 4)
- First convert in Asia (verse 5)
- Worked very hard for others (verse 6)
- Relatives, fellow prisoners who were believers before him (verse 7)
- Whom I love in the Lord (beloved dear friend) (verse 8)
- Tested and approved in Christ (verse 10)
- Member of the household of a friend (verses 10-11)
- Worked hard in the Lord (verse 12)
- One who was like a mother (verse 13)

Each person provoked a specific memory in Paul's mind. They had performed specific acts of help or kindness or friendship. Friendship requires action. Note that these people were often inter-related, not just individuals with independent friendships with Paul. All of these friendships centered around Jesus and His mission. All of these friends were recipients of Paul's love and teaching and sacrifice on their behalf. All were virtuous friendships.

In our early years of marriage, our first three children were almost identical ages to our closest friends at the time, Roger and Joanne. The bonding between us as couples grew as our children related and as we did activities together as families. For several years, we lived within one block of each another, so we had frequent contact. Mary and Joanne talked about the children, homemaking, and hospitality. Jerry and Roger talked about other things, such as grad school, work, and helping Academy cadets. Because our home was small, Jerry needed to convert a corner of the basement to an office. Jerry's abilities in construction are definitely limited, so Roger came with equipment and skill and helped Jerry build bookshelves that have lasted for years and are still in use today. Roger graciously gave his time, knowledge, and ability to build those shelves. He expected nothing in return.

Through the years, we have hosted or led couples' Bible studies. These studies always include about an hour of personal sharing and prayer, followed by an hour of Bible study. Occasionally we spend a weekend away together. In the group, we have encountered struggles with children, career changes, serious illness, and depression. All these experiences have deepened our bonds and given opportunities to serve one another. Once friends open up about their hopes, fears, and anxieties to each other, they form a shared bonding of personal empathy. This is different from getting a prayer request by phone or e-mail, even about someone you know. It is a connection of presence.

Personal touch and personal presence are vital to deep and virtuous friendships. In spite of a plethora of technical means of relating with people (marriage and dating sites, texting, e-mail, Facebook, Twitter, LinkedIn, and so on), deep friendship is not usually developed until people meet face-to-face. Once a friendship has begun, these other means of communication enhance it.

Deep and lasting friendships also develop in the context of serving and relating to others, in community. Such friendships are never isolated; they exist in the context of other friendships and groups of people. When we share a passion for evangelism, orphans, the poor, the homeless, parenting, or education, we form bonds that go beyond self.

For most of our adult lives, we have been passionate about evangelism and discipleship, particularly in our context with The Navigators. It is not surprising that most of our close friends share that passion. We speak the same language and care about people growing deeply into the faith as a disciple.

One stated purpose of our covenant group is "to help each other walk with Jesus for a lifetime." This purpose has taken many forms. We resonate with each other's passions, even critiquing them at times. When we meet as friends, our conversation almost always includes what we are doing or experiencing spiritually. Of course we talk about children, grandchildren, work, health, and our involvement in our local church or community. Spiritual topics are part of an integrated conversation.

We try to practice virtuous friendship not only in our covenant group but in all our relationships. It doesn't come naturally. It requires both an understanding of the nature of virtuous friendship and an intentionality to practice it.

OUR MODEL FOR VIRTUOUS FRIENDSHIP

Jesus spoke often of friendship; He surrounded Himself with friends: He defined the parameters of friendship: He initiated friendship with strangers, and He offered the deepest spiritual truths possible to His friends. He spoke often of love and its place in relationships with other people and with God the Father. He had nothing of monetary value to give to His friends, but He enriched them with His presence, truth, peace, love and finally, His life.

Friendship with Jesus,
Fellowship divine,
Oh, what blessed sweet communion,
Jesus is a friend of mine. — Joseph C. Ludgate

Jesus developed His friendships by being with His friends. During His three years of public ministry, He spent the majority of His time with the twelve disciples. They walked together, talked together, ate together. He taught as He went. His actions demonstrated what He taught. When He healed people or cast out demons, His disciples asked questions about how He was able to do these things. He spoke publically but saved His most intimate conversations for private time with the disciples.

Jesus was patient with His friends, but He still corrected them when He observed issues in their lives or actions. He spoke the truth with love. He could have been incredibly impatient with Thomas, who was a "show me" kind of person (see John 20:25), but He was not. Jesus was loyal to His disciples, even to Judas. He befriended the most unlikely people: Mary Magdalene, who had been demon possessed; Nicodemus, a Pharisee; Zacchaeus, a hated tax collector, even the chief tax collector; the sick and untouchables; a Roman centurion; the Samaritan woman with multiple marriages.

Jesus demonstrated compassion and kindness in all of His relationships. He treated His mother, Mary, with great kindness, leaving a picture of responsibility in the family. He put God, His Father, in the middle of all of His relationships. Jesus was the perfect example of virtuous friendship, and in giving it to others, we can be like Him.

In summing up his idea of friendship and moral virtue, Bennett gave us a clear picture of what virtuous friendship looks like:

Here we find friends who stick together in adversity, friends who give more than they expect to receive, friends who incite each other to higher purposes. We find small deeds done for the sake of friendship, as well as great acts of sacrifice; friends simply going a little out of their way for each other, and friends risking or even offering their lives. We see pleasure found in new friendships, comfort known in old ones, and pain suffered for those lost. From these varieties of friendships, we learn to improve our own.[5]

Virtuous friendship has no equal. Practice it. Reach out to someone who may need your encouragement. Be more of a giver than a receiver. When we give and receive virtuous friendship, what follows brings lifetime value to us and pleasure to us and to God.

THOUGHTS and DISCUSSION

1. How is virtuous friendship different from other or ordinary friendships?

2. How has the discussion of virtuous friendship altered your view of friendship?

3. Write down (or discuss) the instances in which you have practiced virtuous friendship or been the recipient of a virtuous friendship.

4. Think of several friends you have known for more than ten years. By each name, jot a phrase that describes some characteristic or action that ties each of them to you. They may be phrases such as "stuck by me when I was depressed," "challenged me to study the Scriptures," "we traded babysitting, always gracious," "met on the golf course, admired attitude," "met at church and they invited us for lunch," "roommate in college, shared Christ with me." These are specific actions worthy of remembering.

Chapter 5

UNDERSTANDING EACH OTHER

It seems to me that trying to live without friends is like milking a bear to get cream for your morning coffee. It is a whole lot of trouble and then not worth much after you get it.

ZORA NEALE HURSTON

It's beauty that captures your attention; personality which captures your heart.

OSCAR WILDE

Eros will have naked bodies; friendship, naked personalities.

C. S. LEWIS

JERRY ATTENDED A SOCCER game for our granddaughter and saw what looked like our daughter Kris running across the field toward him. He wondered, *Why is my forty-year-old daughter running to jump into my arms?* Then he realized it was Audrey, our granddaughter! Like snowflakes and fingerprints, people may look alike at a distance, but up close, no two are alike—not physically, not emotionally, and not in their personalities. Not even identical twins, similar as they are, lack differences.

More than seven billion people now inhabit our planet, yet God makes each one different from the others. DNA threads that vary just minutely make you who you are: a unique creation of God. Indeed, we are "fearfully and wonderfully made" (Psalm 139:14). It seems impossible that out of billions of people, there are no duplicates, but God's creation teems with originality.

We relish the comfort and security of friends but soon realize the vast differences in each one of them. We've found that when we take into account some of the factors that shape and mold our personalities and behavior, it has helped us better understand, support, and love our friends and family. In order to help you do the same, let's take a closer look at some of those factors.

UNDERSTANDING PERSONALITY DIFFERENCES

Psychologists and sociologists have created various tools to help us assess and describe our personalities. The enneagram offers nine possible categories of personality types.

- Type I—The Need to Be Perfect—Idealists
- Type II—The Need to Be Needed—Caregivers
- Type III—The Need to Succeed—Confident
- Type IV—The Need to Be Special—Sensitive, Artistic
- Type V—The Need to Perceive—Head people, Thinkers
- Type VI—The Need for Security—Team Players
- Type VII—The Need to Avoid Pain—Optimists
- Type VIII—The Need to Be Against—Strong, Reliable
- Type IX—The Need to Avoid—Peacemakers[1]

Understanding our own primary personality characteristic and that of our friends, along with the subcharacteristics we display, gives more understanding and appreciation for who we are, the way God created us, and what we bring to friendships.

Another helpful evaluation tool for understanding personality differences is the Myers-Briggs Type Indicator assessment tool. It categorizes people with sixteen possible indicators of their personalities. The Myers-Briggs has helped marriage partners, friends, and coworkers determine their strengths and weaknesses and understand one another.[2]

Personality definitions are nothing new. From ancient times, great thinkers have tried to explain the human personality. Plato and Aristotle gave it a try. They felt there were four personality types, based on body fluids.

1. Sanguine — sociable and pleasure seeking
2. Choleric — ambitious and leader-like
3. Melancholic — introverted and thoughtful
4. Phlegmatic — relaxed and quiet

Contemporary psychologists and sociologists are still trying to find definitive ways to describe our personalities. Tests and assessments point the way toward understanding ourselves, our families, and our friends, but they do not tell the whole story of one's personality. The part of the story they do tell is important but not complete. We are more complex than can be explained by any test. We all have variations, even when we show characteristics that are most dominant in a particular personality type. Even so, personality tests can help clarify our perception and knowledge of ourselves and others. They can give us an idea of where people are coming from and what valuable contributions they have to make to friendships in general and close friendships specifically.

When we develop friendships, or even romantic interests, it is often with people who demonstrate personality characteristics we ourselves lack. We see things in one another that we would like in ourselves, but because we can't naturally demonstrate those qualities, we often seek them in marriage partners and friends. For instance, Jerry is an extrovert, a leader, decisive, patient, energetic, and competitive. Mary is an introvert, sensitive, thoughtful, orderly, and caring. Opposites do attract, even if the contrasting traits also create conflict and misunderstanding.

Personality types affect our friendships, both positively and negatively. The more we understand the differences in personality types, the more tolerant and understanding we can be of those who are different from us. For example, while the two of us listed only positive qualities about ourselves, we have negative qualities that can create friction between us. Jerry is persistent when he has an idea he wants to promote. Mary can be initially resistant to his notions because they often entail a lot of work, usually on her part. Jerry tends to be casual (shall we say messy?) with housekeeping details in his office and at home. His thought is, *Why mess with stuff if there are people around to relate to?* Mary can be obsessive about tidiness. She thinks order is like cleanliness: next to godliness. These personality tendencies have led to some significant misunderstandings over the years, but understanding each other's personality type has helped us gradually come to a place of acceptance or, sometimes, resignation.

If you use these personality assessment tools, keep a good sense of humor and broad-mindedness. Don't worry about being put into a box. Remember that how you are seen and perceived might not be how you see and perceive yourself.

GETTING TO KNOW EACH OTHER'S PERSONAL HISTORY

Jerry's parents were divorced when he was an infant. Until he was eight, he was raised by his mother and grandfather in a small town in Iowa. He struggled with anxiety when his mother remarried and moved to Spokane, Washington, with a new (and very fine) stepfather. Jerry studied engineering in college and chose an Air Force career but experienced disruption in his career plans.

Mary was a sheltered, red-haired, skinny farm girl raised by a strong, protective father who served as a pastor in small churches. Her mother suffered a twelve-year terminal illness that thrust Mary into a caring role in the family as the eldest daughter.

If, when we met at the University of Washington, we had been able to go to meet each other's families and wander through the rooms we each grew up in, it would have given us some insight into our differences. Looking back, one experience in particular should have given us an early clue. One day Jerry offered Mary a ride to her home in central Washington at the close of the school term, telling her to be packed and ready by a certain time. She was. He arrived late and said he had been a bit too busy to pack. He took her to his college housing residence, where he ran in, returned with dresser drawers, and unceremoniously dumped them in the backseat of the car. Astonished is too mild a word to describe Mary's reaction! But, as the saying goes, "Love is blind." We thought we were quite similar: We both loved God, were focused on our educations, and enjoyed the same people. Little did we realize some major differences.

As the two of us got to know each other's history and met parents and siblings, we began to see how each of us had been shaped. Today, as our friendship grows closer, one of our favorite exercises is to share more of our stories. We continue to find out new things about one another.

Remember how the LORD your God led you all the way.
—*Deuteronomy 8:2*

We often ask our friends to tell us more of their stories, and it opens up hours of tears, laughter, and empathy as we develop our friendships. As we trade stories, we continue to learn about one another and gain new knowledge, appreciation, and understanding. We never fully escape our history. Thank God for both the blessings and the trials. They make you—and your friends—who you are today.

ACCEPTING THE NEED FOR FUNCTIONAL FRIENDSHIPS

Circumstances often connect us with people we would not choose to be friends with if we were not in regular contact with them. Our lives work much better when we accept the need to make these people our friends. We call these relationships "functional friendships" because they fulfill a function in our lives at a certain point in time.

The most obvious kinds of functional friendships are those within our families. For instance, Jerry is the only child of his parents' first marriage, but he relates to half brothers and a half sister, nieces, and nephews from two other marriages. Siblings, aunts, uncles, parents, and cousins are in our lives for a lifetime. Families today can become quite complex with multiple marriages and their resulting complications, and conflicts can easily result. We need to make every effort to develop and maintain friendships within our families. Novels and movies abound depicting conflicts among siblings and relatives. Sorrow and sadness always result. The more we can do to develop friendships in the family, the more satisfying our lives will be. Tolerance and grace will often win the day.

We also develop functional friendships in the context of our jobs. We acquire these friendships so we can do our work better. Sometimes they flourish and develop into lasting friendships, but sometimes they simply serve the purpose of making our work life more enjoyable and the friendship is dropped once our contact with that person is no longer mandatory.

We make functional friendships with our contacts at church, at school, on committees, and in our neighborhoods. The oil of friendship makes our relationships with these people run more smoothly. We need to be able to get along with them, and they need to get along with us. Whether the friendship develops into lifelong friends remains uncertain. What's important is that we accept the need to get along peaceably with certain people.

RECOGNIZING THE VALUE OF CROSS-GENERATIONAL FRIENDSHIPS

Most of us are drawn to people who are at a similar stage of life with similar backgrounds, education, or work. Conceptually, we should relate to any age, but practically, it seldom happens. Several years ago, our church established fellowship groups. Every member received an assignment to a group. First clue of a problem: Our group included a grandmother, parents of teens, a young man just out of the drug culture, and a single woman. That group did not last. You cannot assign relationships. For that reason, when we are inviting people to join our couples' Bible study, we ask ourselves, *Will they relate and connect? Will they share interests? Do they share similar backgrounds?* We include exceptions to this general rule, but commonality usually drives friendship and good group interactions.

Although we relate primarily with people of our own age and stage of life, plus or minus a few years, we want to stress the importance of investing our lives in those who are younger than we are. In the church, we have an incredible opportunity for cross-generation friendships. We discussed cross-age relationships with a group of twentysomething men, and these comments stood out.

- "Well, an older man who is not my dad, who doesn't have a bias, has made all the difference in my life. Just a man who actually cares about my life and about coming alongside me."

- "I am the opposite of you. I don't feel that I find a lot of humility in older men. And I feel there's a lot of talking and not a lot of listening. Maybe it's just our personalities, and that's why it's been so hard to find an older man who I actually respect and who shows me that what he says is more than just words."

- "I guess I feel like a punk kid around older men, like they don't see my heart or understand. They just see my exterior coming from a different generation. 'Oh, he has piercings and a lip ring and his hat's backward. He doesn't love Jesus or he wouldn't do that.' So what frustrates me is that I don't feel there are a whole lot of men who do actually spend time and know the heart."

The two of us have been fortunate to have a few friends ten to twenty years older than we are who cared for and invested in us. Many of our friends over the last twenty years are ten to fifteen years younger. They challenge us and keep us up to date.

Our son, Steve, enjoyed an unusual friendship with his great-grandmother. They held different political views, they were sixty-plus years apart, and they lived in different parts of the country. Steve was her first great-grandchild. She enjoyed being with him and he with her. They could sit quietly together or talk for hours. Steve would drive a long way to see her and they would sit on the porch of her farmhouse enjoying the seasons. They ate at Pizza Hut. They weren't looking for anything beyond the love and enjoyment of one another. They appreciated and accepted their differences.

ACCEPTING OTHERS FOR WHO THEY ARE

Negative or quick judgments about another person can deprive us of some special relationships. Life hammers people so they are affected both in appearance and personality. Divorces, job changes, losses, and hard knocks change who we are. A once-trusting person can become wary and cautious in friendship. All too often, we judge others based on our own preferences and inclinations. If a friend has a rough edge that needs softening or polishing, we criticize and judge that friend or even terminate the friendship. Of course, if this is our response, we miss out on the opportunity to help our friend grow and change in positive ways. The far better way is to extend grace, understanding, and tolerance to friends when they demonstrate traits that irritate us. Jesus offered a wonderful suggestion: "Do not judge, or you too will be judged. For in the same way you judge others, you will be judged, and with the measure you use, it will be measured to you" (Matthew 7:1-2).

On meeting someone, look for the positives in that person. Judgment leads to comparisons. It demeans the other person and causes us to be critical, if not cynical. This practice can be deadly. Almost as deadly is constantly comparing ourselves to others. Comparisons either magnify our flaws or cause us to elevate our good points. Neither helps form or keep healthy friendships.

Judgment is hard to bear when it's true, very painful when it's not true. — *unknown*

CHANGING FOR THE BETTER

When we set out to offer our friendship to someone or respond to his or her overtures to us, we need to consider what we have to contribute to the friendship. Romans 12:3 tells us, "Do not think of yourself more highly than you ought, but rather think of yourself with sober judgment, in accordance with the faith God has distributed to each of you." We don't have to change to be someone's friend, but we do need to understand what qualities we have and not exaggerate or subdue those qualities. Some people concentrate on their weaknesses rather than accepting and being grateful for the good qualities that define their lives. Others magnify their good assets beyond reason and therefore present themselves in a proud and unpleasant way, not realizing the negative aspects of their personalities.

All of us want friends, new and old, to accept us for who we are but always with the understanding that we are working, with God's help, to change for the better. We, and they, are bearers of the image of Christ.

God can use our friends to change us for the better through their love and influence, and we can do the same for them. The Broadway play *Wicked* produced some lovely songs. The lyrics of "For Good" speak beautifully to the idea that friends change us: "Who can say if I've been changed for the better? But because I knew you, I have been changed for good."[3]

We're all changing and growing, with God's help, in constructive ways. He will bring people through our lives who bring us closer to Him and to one another and who change us in remarkable ways. Our personalities are refined as we walk with Jesus and let His Spirit change us.

When our covenant group began meeting many years ago, we were in our thirties and forties. The youngest among us was still in her twenties. We all had some rough edges that needed smoothing. We seldom hesitated to point out the failures to one another, sometimes with heightened emotions and raised voices. At one point during a heated exchange, Mary, usually verbally restrained, told another group member he was acting like a horse's patootie! Later she apologized and asked his forgiveness. Rarely do such interactions take place now. We have grown spiritually; we have increased in love for one another, and our conversations are far more moderate. Plus, the Lord is changing us into the people He wants us to be:

"If anyone is in Christ, the new creation has come: The old has gone, the new is here!" (2 Corinthians 5:17).

The French phrase *vive la différence* can be translated, "Long live the difference" (between genders). So it is with friends. What a boring life it would be if we were all the same. As we build our friendships, let's set aside our expectation that everyone be like us. Let's be patient with one another and take time to build a shared history so that we might know and understand each other.

We love the beauty of Margery Williams' conversation between the Rabbit and the Skin Horse as they discuss love in *The Velveteen Rabbit*.

"Real isn't how you are made," said the Skin Horse. "It's a thing that happens to you. When a child loves you for a long, long time, not just to play with, but REALLY loves you, then you become Real."

"Does it hurt?" asked the Rabbit.

"Sometimes," said the Skin Horse, for he was always truthful. "When you are Real you don't mind being hurt."

"Does it happen all at once, like being wound up," he asked, "or bit by bit?"

"It doesn't happen all at once," said the Skin Horse.

"You become. It takes a long time. That's why it doesn't happen often to people who break easily, or have sharp edges, or who have to be carefully kept. Generally, by the time you are Real, most of your hair has been loved off, and your eyes drop out and you get loose in the joints and very shabby.

"But these things don't matter at all, because once you are Real you can't be ugly, except to people who don't understand."[4]

Like the Skin Horse, we are formed by the beautiful differences and loving attention of our friends, and we help form them. They tolerate and even appreciate our eccentricities. They love us for who we are, not for who they want us to be. In their presence, we feel acceptance and encouragement. Even when there is correction or critique, we receive it, knowing they have our best interests at heart. Our personality differences complement and even challenge one another.

Let's be real; let's seek to understand each other.

THOUGHTS and DISCUSSION

1. Discuss the extent to which personality plays in your friendships.
2. What, if any, are the implications of the Hurston quote at the beginning of this chapter?
3. How is your history affecting the way you approach friendships?
4. Who do you have functional friendships with?

Chapter 6

HOW MUCH DOES FRIENDSHIP COST?

A friend is one who walks in when others walk out.

WALTER WINCHELL

Time is the most valuable thing that we have because it
is the most irrevocable.

DIETRICH BONHOEFFER

EVERYONE LOOKS AT PRICE tags. We want to know what
something will cost us, yet all of us have certain things for which,
for various reasons—prestige, enjoyment, or vanity—we are willing to pay more. Cost and affordability relate directly to our value
systems. Some people show financial extravagance in automobile
purchases, furniture and home decorations take prime importance
for some, and still others are most into the latest in clothing styles,
hair fashion, and jewelry.

Most newly married couples experience conflict due to differing values. This was true for us. Even when we barely had two dimes
to rub together, our spending preferences were at odds. An engineer,

Jerry favored getting the best electronics available; Mary wanted to expand the grocery bill.

Another issue that brought up financial discussions in our home was our daughters' love of horses. Anyone who has owned a horse knows that the initial purchase price is only a small part of the real cost. Feed, veterinarian fees, and boarding make up the real ongoing cost. We were never able to afford a horse, but a number of times, horses were loaned to our girls on a temporary basis. We paid the costs while the horses were with us.

Friendships, too, have a cost attached to them, which is one reason we can sustain only so many at any one time. Our capacity is limited, especially for intimate friendships. One of the ongoing discussions in our marriage revolves around how many relationships we can sustain as a couple. Mary, as an introvert, focuses on fewer friends and more depth in the relationship. Jerry, as an extrovert, gathers relationships by the dozens. The conflict comes when we as a couple try to integrate them. When forming friendships, we usually do not initially back away because of a perceived cost, yet it does become a factor as we choose whether to commit to a deeper friendship.

IDENTIFYING AND PRIORITIZING THE COST

Have you ever looked at your caller ID as you received a phone call and thought, *I just don't have time or energy to talk to that person right now?* and then let the call go to voice mail? You're not alone. Everyone has done this at some time. On the other hand, we immediately answer the call from certain people, even if it is 2:00 a.m. Both calls bear a cost to us, but the difference in response is the depth and commitment of the relationship.

So what are the costs in a friendship, and how might we prioritize them as we progress in deepening a friendship?

Time

Every phone call, text, e-mail, and face-to-face meeting takes time, and time is one irreplaceable commodity we have. This is not news to you. You either choose to make time, choose not to make time, or choose to limit your time.

At times, special circumstances arise in the lives of our friends, calling for our time. When the needs of our friends and family are acute, we move them to the top of our priority list. We did this recently because one of our close friends was dying. We dropped everything to be with the family in her last days. We were privileged to stand with her extended family as she took her last breath and entered eternity, a hallowed moment we were fortunate to share. Several years ago, when one of our daughters experienced surgery with complications, our schedules turned to lifting her load with her children and meeting her physical needs. We watched her friends also surround her with love and help, standing by her hospital bed and praying as she suffered, taking her children to school, cleaning her house, and supplying an endless stream of delicious meals. All of these efforts required much time from her friends.

When suffering invades a friend's life—whether from a death in the family, a personal health issue, a child in difficulty, or some other traumatic event—we must consider the extent to which we should become involved. Will we change plans to be present when a friend needs us? Over the years, we have resolved to respond immediately to the needs of friends who are not believers and to make time for them. We give them priority because we want to demonstrate the love of Jesus to them.

Energy and Effort

Every relationship requires energy and effort, of which we have limited amounts. We cannot do everything and respond to everyone. The balance between work, family, and selected friends requires constant choices. Don't beat yourself up when you wear out. Give yourself freedom to say no.

We have friends who are quick to respond to the needs of others. When they are depleted of energy, they announce, "We're canceling the weekend!" Without guilt, they wipe the calendar clean for a few days to restore their energy. They wisely recognize they cannot help others if they are exhausted. They make it a priority to guard their health so they have more to give to others.

Every relationship requires energy and effort, of which we have limited amounts. We cannot do everything and respond to everyone.

We have all been told that people need to work on their marriages by giving them attention, effort, and priority. The same holds true for friendships. We need to be intentional in their development and priority. This is particularly true for the ten to twenty close relationships that are current and active in our lives right now.

Keep in mind that some relationships build you up and others drain you. The relationships that give us great pleasure take little energy and effort to develop. The ones that drain us have a higher cost, but our commitment to the friendship may draw us to pay the price. Friendships and the costs incurred in them ebb and flow throughout the years. In close and intimate relationships, we remain loyal and committed, even if the friendship shifts to being more difficult than it once was.

Vulnerability

Webster's dictionary defines *vulnerable* as "capable of being physically or emotionally wounded; open to attack or damage." Its synonyms are "endangered, exposed, open, sensitive."

Given these definitions, who would ever want to be vulnerable?

It is difficult. Opening up your heart and soul to another is uncomfortable. Yet when you do, burdens and anxiety can be eased. Galatians 6:2 says, "Carry each other's burdens, and in this way you will fulfill the law of Christ." This passage is in the context of restoring those who have sinned, but it applies more broadly to the law of Christ as the law of love. When we go through difficult times, we need others to help us carry our burdens, and we need to do the same for them.

We do not wait until a crisis to open up and call friends for help, particularly in the area of accountability. An early foundation of openness and vulnerability sets the stage for asking for help before a crisis occurs.

Men, do you ever discuss the issue of sexual temptation with a close male friend? Have you shared your struggles with pornography? How about your insecurities at work? Have you ever asked for help in your walk with Jesus? Having close friends can make it safe to bring up the real issues of life.

Women, do you discuss your fear for your children or frustrations in raising teens? Have you discussed issues of identity, how you look, or tension in your marriage? How about struggles in your workplace? What about sexual temptation for yourself, your husband, or your children?

Are you willing to pay the cost of being vulnerable with your close friends? Vulnerability may bring the added costs of embarrassment, shame, and the difficulty of sharing personal struggles. That is why discretion needs to be used when we're vulnerable. We should share confidences with only close, safe friends, not casual friends or acquaintances. A safe friend is someone who has proven reliable with love and confidentiality. If you discuss intimate matters with an untested acquaintance, it can lead to disillusionment, deep hurt, and embarrassment. At times, people use a counselor to reveal their deepest needs because they know that counselors must adhere to severe restrictions on confidentiality.

Take the risk; test the waters. When we pay the cost of vulnerability in a close friendship, we break out of superficial facade and the "Everything is just fine, thank you" syndrome.

We should share confidences with only close, safe friends, not casual friends or acquaintances. A safe friend is someone who has proven reliable with love and confidentiality. If you discuss intimate matters with an untested acquaintance, it can lead to disillusionment, deep hurt, and embarrassment.

Unanticipated and Unplanned Costs

Old Testament figures David and Jonathan were the closest of friends. They pledged both loyalty and lifelong commitment to each other. Jonathan was King Saul's son and heir to the throne of Israel. When God rejected Saul because of his disobedience, Saul turned against David, doggedly trying to kill him. Even though Saul had brought David into his court, as soon as he became a threat, Saul did all he could to kill him.

In anger, Saul yelled at Jonathan, "You son of a perverse and rebellious woman! Don't I know that you have sided with the son of Jesse [David] to your own shame and to the shame of the mother who bore you? As long as the son of Jesse lives on this earth, neither you nor your kingdom will be established. Now send someone to bring him to me, for he must die!" (1 Samuel 20:30-31). Jonathan refused to give David over to Saul. He kept his friendship with David, knowing it would cost him the throne.

When Jonathan told David about Saul's plans to kill him,

David got up from his hiding place beside the boulder, then fell on his face to the ground—three times prostrating himself! And then they kissed one another and wept, friend over friend, David weeping especially hard.

Jonathan said, "Go in peace! The two of us have vowed friendship in GOD's name, saying, 'GOD will be the bond between me and you, and between my children and your children forever!'" (verses 41-42, MSG)

We must not distort this passage with sexual connotations. This was true, godly friendship. Jonathan and David pledged friendship to each other and their families forever. They never saw one another again. Seeing God's hand on David, Jonathan gave up his future and kept his pledge of friendship. Years later, David returned that friendship by showing kindness to Jonathan's crippled son, Mephibosheth. He brought him into his court, supported him financially, and returned family property to him (see 2 Samuel 9).

We may never pay a price like that for our friendship, but there will be costs that we did not and could not anticipate:

- In the corporate world, we see people withdrawing from someone else when that person is being criticized, attacked, and even dismissed. They do not want to get caught in the cross fire. The same holds true in the political realm. Will you stand up for others, especially when they are your friends?
- When you are discussing spiritual truths with someone, you might discover unanticipated issues that require you to help the person in both personal and family life. Will you come to the rescue, spiritually and emotionally, if needed?
- Sin invades everyone's life. When sin issues burst into the open, we are all impacted. Are you willing to become involved in confronting, helping, and healing?
- When a friend is suffering, will you change plans to be available to help? Will you respond to the need and become involved?

When our son died, a friend of ours appeared at our daughter's door, in another city, with airline tickets in hand to travel with her to meet us in Colorado Springs. We discovered only later the unexpected costs of time, energy, effort, and money our friend expended, expecting nothing in return. This was a beautiful example of virtuous friendship.

It can be easy to sacrifice our time and energy for our closest friends. It is quite another matter to do so for acquaintances and casual friends. But remember, every relationship must have virtuous elements. We give, expecting nothing in return. We gladly pay the cost out of commitment and love.

When Jesus healed the blind man in John 9, the man had no idea who Jesus was. In fact, Jesus often avoided being known. Let's serve our friends in the same selfless way.

THOUGHTS and DISCUSSION

1. Why is friendship costly?
2. Given your personality, age, and experience, what about being vulnerable is difficult for you?
3. What differences in vulnerability do you observe between men and women?
4. How has suffering impacted the cost in your friendships?

Chapter 7

TEXTING, TECHNOLOGY, AND FRIENDSHIP

Let's say you are going to a party, so you pull out some pocket change and buy a little greeting card that plays "Happy Birthday" when it's open. After the party, someone casually tosses the card into the trash, throwing away more computer power than existed in the entire world before 1950.

JOHN HUEY

They're texting. They're instant messaging. They're texting while instant messaging.

ROBIN MEJIA

ENIAC, COMMONLY THOUGHT OF as the first modern computer, was built in 1944. It took up more space than an eighteen-wheel tractor trailer, weighed more than seventeen Chevrolet Camaros, and consumed 140,000 watts of electricity.

In 1970, when completing his PhD dissertation, Jerry used an early Burroughs computer for his research in astronautics. The computer was a great, hulking thing that took up space in an entire room. Many people worked on it, and each was assigned a certain time slot. Jerry's scheduled time was in the middle of the night, and he had exclusive use of the computer. He took those hours of computer time, as it was his only option. Today the same program would run on an average laptop computer.

We acquired our first personal computer in 1982. It was little more than an improved word processor with, of course, no access to the Internet, which had yet to be developed. Our introduction to the new technology amazed us, and we felt the ultimate in electronics had been achieved.

When Mary bought her first iPod several years ago, she was baffled by the process of downloading music and movies. Our ten-year-old granddaughter came to our home, adjusted a few inputs, clicked a few buttons, and the job was done. Mary had to ask her to repeat the process more slowly so she could learn to do it herself. She realized then that constant learning would be essential to keeping up with the digital developments happening so quickly.

Our eleven grandchildren are technologically adept. If we want to communicate with them, we must be adept also. Their generation does not write letters. Few know the price of a postage stamp. They view phone landlines as antiques. Our communication with them is and will be by text messages, FaceTime, tweets, and whatever technologies are developed in the future.

In 2001, Marc Prensky coined the terms *digital natives* and *digital immigrants*. Digital natives have used technology almost since their infancy. Many of their earliest toys use simple electronic systems. They are not intimidated by technology and use it to every advantage. Digital immigrants are playing catch-up and find new technology confusing and daunting. However, they must become more comfortable with it because it is here to stay and growing at a rapid rate.

No one would argue that Smartphones, iPads, and the many devices we have access to have made our lives easier and more entertaining for our kids. But technology has drastically changed family life as well. — *Julie Revelant*

When we look back over the centuries, we see that there have always been alternatives to voice-to-voice, face-to-face communication. Trumpets, smoke signals, flags, whistles, and drums have conveyed messages from one person to another, from one group to another, and these messages had to be succinct and brief. These message forms were primitive but effective. In Joshua 6, the Israelites conquered the city of Jericho. When the Israelites marched around the city for six days, the city's residents knew that something ominous was about to happen. But when on the seventh day they heard the trumpets blowing and the marchers gave a tremendous shout, they knew that disaster had arrived. Communication without words.

What is friendship like in the digital era? How does the rise of technology affect our relationships? Or does it? The simple answer is yes, which is why we need to understand the downside and the upside of digital communication and social media in our friendships.

THE DOWNSIDE OF DIGITAL COMMUNICATION

It's becoming more common for people to use an electronic device to communicate rather than to have a personal conversation. For example:

- At a recent dinner of a dozen people, everyone at the table but the grandmother was consulting their cell phones between the main course and dessert. Grandma sat alone and ignored while the techies checked their messages, tweets, and texts. When the desserts arrived, down went the cell phones, and conversation resumed.

- A pastor was speaking on Sunday morning. Midway through his sermon he stopped and asked, "How many of you have texted or consulted your cell phones since I started speaking?" About 40 percent of the congregation readily admitted their cell phone use.

- A young man in his twenties told us, "I use Facebook, Twitter, texting, all that. I happen to be a little lazy and it takes a lot of work to actually have to talk to someone on the phone, but I can text as I am watching TV. It's quick, but at the same time, you don't do what it takes to build deep or important friendships." Even though this young man recognized the limitations to building friendships through technology, it was his preferred mode of communication with his friends.

Many people are becoming indifferent to making an effort for personal contact and instead are relying on impersonal gadgets to maintain their relationships. The conveniences are great, but so also are the risks. Communicating electronically may temporarily fill a void, but in the end it leaves only emptiness and frustration. One young introvert told us, "I love it when my phone breaks. That's the best time of my life because all of a sudden, I'm not always on call." Another said, "The only issue with texting and Facebooking is that you don't have facial cues and body language, so you don't know what the person really means, like if they're being sarcastic or what."

Digital communication is no substitute for personal time with friends. Even so, some people would rather spend hours on the computer communicating with unseen, unknown people than spend time with friends. The hazards of this interaction can lead to disastrous disappointment, even social and physical harm, for anyone can throw up a pretense on electronic communication. Criminals and frauds can assume any pose and lure innocent people into dangerous situations.

Some people are so enamored of the varied uses of digital communication that their real lives become submerged by their electronic pursuits — playing games, collecting information, following news minutia, and other potentially wasteful activities. This was the case for Mike. A recent graduate from a prestigious university with a degree in computer science, he was well aware of the capacity and complexities of digital communication. Although recently married, he spent little time with his wife. Instead, he remained glued to his computer, communicating with people he had never met, reading endless reports on obscure information that would never be of practical use. Gradually, his friends drifted away and his wife declared a separation if he couldn't drag himself away from the computer. This proved to be a wake-up call for Mike. Realizing the disastrous nature of his addiction, he removed his computer from his home and used a computer only at work. This radical action saved his marriage, and gradually his friendships resumed.

Equally concerning, some research indicates that excessive digital interruptions reduce brain attention by 20 percent. This is alarming given the amount of time most of us spend on computers and cell phones. We would be wise to learn to control and manage digital communication to our best advantage.

THE UPSIDE OF DIGITAL COMMUNICATION

The question is, how can we use electronic communication to its best advantage in our friendships while avoiding the consequences of squandered hours with Smartphone or computer in hand?

Used well, digital communication enriches our relationships with our friends. It's new, it's changing, and it's useful. How many times have you thought, *I should give Anne a call,* but then realized that a short phone call when you were busy would not be appropriate. So instead you text her and get an almost immediate reply. She knows you are thinking about her. Then, when both of you have more time, you can have a longer phone conversation or meet face-to-face.

One way to use digital communication well is to understand that personal contact takes precedence over digital contact. Consider banning the use of digital communications during meals and family time. If you are with a friend, don't text or use the phone unless it is urgent. Mary often has lunch with a friend who understands how to use digital communication in a way that serves her friendships. This friend always asks permission to consult her phone if it buzzes and she is expecting some necessary communication from her children. She ignores all other calls. She has established boundaries for her cell phone use.

We cannot roll back society's constant use of voice and digital communication, but we can put some reasonable limits on it out of consideration of our friends and others. If movie theaters, airplanes, restaurants, courtrooms, concert halls, business meetings, and other public places insist on silencing and turning off digital communication, surely we can do the same in the presence of a friend. That's what voice mail is for!

IF JESUS WERE LIVING TODAY

It is interesting to speculate about whether the current social media would change Jesus' ministry. We believe that it would, but only in His use of how He communicated with His disciples. Personal relational encounters would still be His method of ministry. He would still spend His time with people in small groups and occasionally large crowds. Jesus knew the value of face-to-face speech, eye contact, and touch. Personal contact enabled Him to demonstrate the love of the Father and the purpose for His life on earth.

When His disciples tried to dismiss the children who were crowding around Jesus, He told them, "'Let the little children come to me, and do not hinder them, for the kingdom of heaven belongs to such as these.' When he had placed his hands on them, he went on from there" (Matthew 19:14-15). Jesus knew their innocent faith, their vulnerability, and their desire to be acknowledged and loved. He knew their significance and welcomed and touched them, or, as another translation suggests, "blessed" them (NLT). It's hard to imagine Jesus' sending children an e-mail or text. He wanted them to feel accepted, loved, and important in His personal presence. Children—in fact, all people—value personal attention and contact. There is a language beyond words that communicates to our friends—a warm look, a gentle touch, a quiet presence. Nonverbal communication undergirds all friendships.

Technology cannot warm our hearts, listen to our dreams or troubles, cheer us on in our successes, or comfort us in grief and pain.

HERE TO STAY

We are most likely in the infancy of digital communication. It is burgeoning and here to stay. It will become more powerful and invasive as new technologies are developed. We must adapt with the developments but not allow them to replace personal, face-to-face friendships. As life becomes more complicated and busy, digital resources can help us efficiently manage our lives, but we must not allow them to diminish our friendships, which are vital to our social and spiritual well-being. Friendships provide the lifeblood that sustains our spiritual and emotional souls. Technology cannot warm our hearts, listen to our dreams or troubles, cheer us on in our successes, or comfort us in grief and pain. Let's use it to its best advantage, keeping in mind the value of face-to-face relationships.

THOUGHTS and DISCUSSION

1. How has technology impacted your friendships?
2. Choose and discuss the following descriptive words as they relate to the impact of technology on your friendships:
   Broadened
   Normal
   Narrowed
   Complicated
   Made easier
   Frustrating
3. What are you learning about how to use social media well in your friendship circles? Compare texting and social media to face-to-face connection. Is face-to-face more or less important now?

Chapter 8

THE PAYOFF FOR US AND FOR THEM

It's the friends you can call at 4 a.m. that matter.

MARLENE DIETRICH

I value the friend who for me finds time on his calendar,
but I cherish the friend who for me does not consult his
calendar.

ROBERT BRAULT

THE POWERBALL LOTTERY JUST went over $600 million.
Spend one dollar and get $600 million. What a payoff! The prob-
lem is, you can't get something for nothing. Life doesn't work that
way. Neither does friendship. In friendship, there are times when we
are the receiver, benefiting in ways we can never pay back, and times
when we are the giver, the experience expanding our hearts and
souls.

In this chapter, we want to look at what we get and what we
give in friendship—the benefits we receive from our friends and
the benefits we give to them.

WHAT DO YOU GAIN?

When we asked people about the rewards of friendship, people not only spoke of the benefits of friendships but also the context and variations of friendships. Here are just a few of the varied responses we received:

- "Deep friendship is a safe place."
- "Deep friendship is where you can be yourself and not have to put up the phony exteriors that we tend to put up daily to survive in the workplace. It's like coming home, putting on your favorite slippers, and sitting on the couch—just being who you are."
- "I am drawn to people who are life-givers. When you're in their presence, they are life-givers—teaching me how to play or laugh more or even know how to weep or struggle with my confusion."
- "God cares about relationships—with Him and with each other. Every good relationship is a gift from God. I become more Christlike when friends around the table confront me if I become out of balance or say something stupid."
- "I want to stay young—to stay relevant. Every younger person in your life is a gift from God because of the energy he or she has."
- "If you want to stay young, you need every age in your life. Age-graded Sunday schools were a bad idea. Age-graded life is a bad idea."

Above-mentioned phrases such as "comfortable slippers," "life-givers," "gift from God," and "safe place" reflect a positive and deep emotional response to friendship. Not every friendship evokes such positive responses, yet every friendship contributes to a God-planted need inside us that longs to be nurtured by loving friends.

The rewards of friendship cannot be quantified, yet they can be perceived in their many forms and benefits. We have already talked about some of these benefits, but they bear repeating here.

Enjoyment and Pleasure

Laughter and seriousness are equally present in friendship. Friends look forward to being together. We see this especially in the fifteen-to-thirty-year-old crowd. Observe how they hang out together and run in groups. It is common for them to sit around talking and laughing, watching a movie until three in the morning. Being together is a high priority. In defining her group of friends, a twenty-two-year-old said, "On the one hand, you don't want to be a clique, but on the other hand, you look at Jesus calling just the twelve He grew close to."

As we mature, we value our friends more and more. Shared experiences build a foundation for simple enjoyment and connecting. After his retirement, a friend of ours — a lifetime farmer — met friends every morning at McDonald's for coffee to discuss everything from world politics to the weather to the modern methods of farming. They laughed often even in the midst of good-natured complaints about the current generation of farmers.

There are no friends like the old friends. — James Joyce

Jerry's grandmother lived to be almost ninety-three. One of the most difficult things for her was that almost all of her friends had died before she did. She desperately missed the camaraderie and enjoyment of her lifelong friends. At every age, the pleasure and delight of friendships brings enrichment and satisfaction to our lives.

Help in Time of Need

"Better is a neighbor [friend] who is near than a brother far away" (Proverbs 27:10, NASB). We all need somewhere to turn for help. Friends see our need and come to our rescue. "A friend is always loyal, and a brother is born to help in time of need" (17:17, NLT). People gain great pleasure in helping friends during times of need. It is a blessing, not a burden.

At one point in our lives, we were living very frugally. Dinner menus were limited and simple. Then friends who owned a farm called and said, "Could you use half a beef?" Their unexpected generosity gave us some wonderful dinners and touched us deeply.

There was a man all alone; he had neither son nor brother. There was no end to his toil, yet his eyes were not content with his wealth. "For whom am I toiling," he asked, "and why am I depriving myself of enjoyment?" This too is meaningless—a miserable business! Two are better than one, because they have a good return for their labor: If either of them falls down, one can help the other up. But pity anyone who falls and has no one to help them up. Also, if two lie down together, they will keep warm. But how can one keep warm alone? Though one may be overpowered, two can defend themselves. A cord of three strands is not quickly broken. —Ecclesiastes 4:8-12

Protection

Protection from what? From sin, immorality, and foolish decisions. However, not all friends have your best interests at heart. Wrong friends can lead you the wrong way. "Do not be misled: 'Bad company corrupts good character'" (1 Corinthians 15:33). Choosing the right friends gives you incredible protection. They can give you a sense of spiritual and emotional security. You can trust yourself to close, proven friends.

In 1990, our thirty-year-old son, Steve, was murdered while working at his job as a cab driver. As we grieved his death, both of us experienced a level of depression. Jerry especially sensed regrets about what he had not done with Steve. These thoughts were not rational or even true, but they persisted. Close friends confronted us with the concept of believing lies. They walked us through a process of factual evaluation and of understanding both God's sovereignty and the actual truth. This confrontation protected us from spiraling into self-condemnation and regret.

An Example for Our Children

Our friends have had an enormous influence on our children, even becoming their confidants. When kids see and admire our friends, they start looking for similar kinds of people in their own lives.

Each of our children has significantly benefited from the depth and quality of the friends who have surrounded us from the early days of our marriage. Here's just one example. During her university days, one daughter tired of the chaos of dorm life and the hectic pace of studies. Friends of ours invited her to live with them for a semester, and their love and the peaceful atmosphere in their home rejuvenated and refreshed her.

A NETWORKING PATHWAY

Often the way of the business world is to network your contacts to further your career or finances. Friends can steer us to ethical people who are able to help us in life and business. In times of need or crisis, a network of friends opens many doors. Former classmates, roommates, and work-related friends often respond to a need for help in ways others do not.

We have often seen this in our friends who are physicians. They have been of immeasurable help both for us and our Navigator missionaries in remote areas — for counsel, for knowing the right specialists, and for medical expertise. When our daughter gave birth to her third baby, something did not heal properly, leaving her in incredible pain. We called a friend who was a fellow Air Force officer and doctor. His specialty is obstetrics and gynecology. He examined our daughter, found the problem, and did surgery immediately, bringing healing and relief.

Similarly, one of our closest friends, a medical doctor and nephrologist, found a rare benign tumor on Mary's adrenal gland, the first he had seen in his career. Mary's blood pressure had been climbing for several years to a dangerously high level. In desperation, we had called our friend for help. Subsequent surgery corrected the problem, and we have been so grateful. Sharing networks and friends gives joy and satisfaction.

A Safety Net

In reality, this is what the local church — the community of believers — is supposed to be. In larger congregations, networking takes place in small groups. This safety net is not foolproof or complete, but if you build this circle of friends, it is present and available. The net is built over time and nurtured with care.

Sadly, not everyone has this safety net. Maybe from independence or lack of appreciation for its value, many live without a significant network of friends. It is never too late. Start now.

WHAT DO I HAVE TO GIVE?

We are human, always bending toward self-centeredness, even in the best of friendships. We have limited time, resources, and emotions, so we pick and choose how we will spend those things in friendship. In that process, over time and under God's providential direction, we bond with a relatively small number of people, though we touch many and many touch us.

So what do you have to give that will benefit your friends?

Time

This is one of the most important treasures you can give your friends. When you drop everything to spend time with them, you are telling your friends that you love and care about them and that they are a priority in your life. You are saying, "I am here for you. You are important to me."

Mary recently gave this gift to a friend who had stopped by our home to drop off an item. She stayed and talked with Mary for two hours on issues of deep importance. In tears, she detailed a difficult family situation. She wasn't looking for advice; she simply needed a hearing.

For a number of years, Jerry has left his office door open unless he is in a meeting that demands confidentiality. The happenstance conversations that occur with people dropping by lead to many significant interactions.

Years ago when Jerry served as an Air Force general, he walked into the reception area outside his office and saw a colonel he knew. Jerry asked him how things were going, just a normal in-passing greeting. The colonel said, "Not too well." Then he said those all-important words: "Have you got a minute?" They talked and it led to a life-changing conversation. The colonel's wife had just left him. He told Jerry that after his previous promotion party, his employees talked about what a great boss he was and how he was always there for them. When the colonel and his wife returned home, she asked him, "Why don't you do that for me?" and she left him. He was shaken. He drastically changed his work schedule and priorities and won his wife back, but it was a two-year journey.

Give friends your time. Be generous. Be sensitive. Allow interruptions. Be there. Listen. Pay attention.

Resources

Lucy Sanny—wife of Jerry's predecessor in The Navigators, Lorne Sanny—was a frequent buyer at auctions and garage sales. This was not a shopping addiction; she generously and consistently purchased items for returning missionaries who had little in the way of household goods when they came home from overseas.

Generosity needs to be a way of life no matter what the level of resources one possesses. The apostle Paul wrote, "Command those who are rich in this present world not to be arrogant nor to put their hope in wealth, which is so uncertain, but to put their hope in God, who richly provides us with everything for our enjoyment. Command them to do good, to be rich in good deeds, and to be generous and willing to share" (1 Timothy 6:17-18).

Our family has often been the beneficiary of other people's generosity. For example, when we were led to join The Navigators fulltime with no guaranteed salary, we told our children, "Well, we might have to tighten our belts." One said, "Dad, I don't think I want to tighten my belt." Later that daughter said, "If God is leading my parents, He's leading me." Within the next year, a friend invited our entire family to a five-star guest ranch for a week without cost and did so for the next several years. The value of that week was equivalent to several months' salary for us. Our friends generously blessed us.

Another time, our daughter Karen and her youth pastor husband needed a car. Their resources were limited, as he served in a small church. One of our friends found out about their need and gave them their car since they were buying a new one. This kindness revealed true friendship to us, and beyond us, to our family.

Respect and Encouragement

Your friends are special people, created and loved by God, and, as such, deserving of respect for their person, intellect, spirituality, and even fears and anxieties. As they reveal their deepest secrets, they need both attentiveness and encouragement. Be sensitive to feelings of shame, as shame often causes people to shut down and fear revealing who they really are or what they have done. In Jesus' conversation with the Samaritan woman at the well, He showed incredible respect yet spoke truth (see John 4). Like Jesus, we can do both.

They say a person needs just three things to be happy in their world: someone to love, something to do, and something to hope for. — Tom Bodett

Above all, extend love—unconditional love—to your friends. Love, expecting nothing in return. The two of us are struck by the truth of John 15:13: "Greater love has no one than this: to lay down one's life for one's friends." This is the ultimate example of virtuous friendship.

No friend is perfect. They will sin; they will offend you. That is when they most want and need your love.

Hope

We all live by hope, and friends help friends keep hope. We know that God is the source of all hope. Placing hope anywhere else is futile. But God can use you as a channel for hope—by your love, presence, words, by belief in your friends and by giving them your respect and supporting them both physically and emotionally. God takes the frailty of our humanity and uses it in the life of another.

We have been the recipients of this gift many times. One friend used to call Mary and say, "I have a verse for you," and then quote the verse and say no more. Another often left a Scripture verse and blessing on our voice mail. Our covenant group, time after time, counseled, confronted, and encouraged us. They always left us with hope. Similarly, we are a part of giving hope to the other couples when they need it.

Hope is the thing with feathers that perches in the soul and sings the tune without the words and never stops at all. — Emily Dickinson

We gain and we give. We gain what we do not expect or deserve. We give what cannot be bought. In that giving, we find the purest of gold and the satisfaction that engulfs our souls in the pleasure of friendship.

THOUGHTS and DISCUSSION

1. What is the payoff you get from friendship?
2. What are the ethical boundaries in networking your friendships?
3. How does friendship give you security?
4. Discuss the specific gains and gives in your friendships.

Chapter 9

MEN AND WOMEN: ANY DIFFERENCE?

Marriages are made in heaven. So are thunder and lightning!

UNKNOWN

Men and women belong to different species, and communication between them is still in its infancy.

BILL COSBY

HERE'S AUTHOR BETTY MACDONALD'S take on how men's and women's friendships differ:

Men are so much less demanding in friendship. A woman wants her friends to be perfect. She sets a pattern, usually a reasonable facsimile of herself, lays a friend out on this pattern and worries and prods at any little qualities which do not coincide with her own image. She simply won't be bothered with anything less than ninety percent congruity only if the other ten percent is shaping up nicely and promises accurate conformity within a short time. Friends with glaring lumps or unsmoothable rough places are cast off like ill-fitting garments, and even if this means that the woman has no friends at all, she seems happier than with some imperfect being for whom she would have to make allowances.

A man has a friend, period. He acquires this particular friend because they both like to hunt ducks. The fact that the friend discourses entirely in four letter words, very seldom washes, chews tobacco and spits at random, is drunk a good deal of the time and hates women, in no way affects the friendship. If the man notices these flaws in the perfection of his friend, he notices them casually as he does his friend's height, the color of his eyes, the width of his shoulders; and the friendship continues at an even temperature for years and years and years.[1]

The obvious exaggerations in this excerpt are for humorous effect, but the point remains: Men and women generally conduct their friendships in different ways.

THE DIFFERENCES

A close friend put it succinctly: "Women talk; men do stuff." Women enjoy face-to-face conversations over a lunch table, in lawn chairs on a patio, in comfortable living room chairs. They like to talk and talk and talk. They make eye contact and observe facial expressions, looking for clues to the emotions and feelings of their friends.

One of the most loving relationships between women is recorded in the book of Ruth. Ruth chronicles more personal conversations than most other Bible books. What kinds of things did Ruth and Naomi talk about as they traveled from Moab to Israel? They likely discussed their difficult situation. They talked about their grief, strategic plans, God, and their love for one another. Although they were from different generations and different cultures, their love drew them together into a strong bond.

Men also talk face-to-face with each other but usually at work or during specific activities. Most men converse best side by side, on the golf course, at a car show, in a boat fishing, at a church function, or at a baseball game. They typically avoid drama and neediness in their friendships and are less likely than women to display emotion. They seem to be less judgmental toward their friends than women tend to be and are accepting of deficits in their friends without complaint. As male friendships deepen beyond casual and toward close, the differences between men and women's friendships diminish. Men talk more with their friends as the friendship develops, but often it is still in the context of an activity.

With children, we see these gender distinctions quite clearly. When our kids were young, we often said, "Boys wrestle; girls giggle." Little girls hold hands and talk and talk and talk, often in parallel conversations that have significance for them but no one else. Little boys beyond the toddler age don't hold hands with anyone. They wrestle and tumble and run and climb. Talking seems a waste of time when you could be active.

Through the teenage years, friendship allegiances can change quickly, especially with girls. Their emotions can flare out of control, and they sometimes hold grudges and spread rumors. Many seek the top spot in friendship circles, even if that means hurting others, which is why we hear of "mean girls." These positions are important for supposed respect, confidence, dominance. Teenage boys settle differences physically through some pushing and shoving, rough language, and sports battles. But through all this, boys and girls alike learn what works in relationships, what gives satisfaction, and what brings hurt and disappointment. Through all the relational chaos of the teen years, they learn what to value and what to discard in order to make their friendships constructive and beneficial. As they enter adulthood, their friendship styles should have matured so that they can find satisfying relationships in which they can give and receive support, love, and enjoyment.

Of course, there are exceptions. Similarities exist between the sexes; we are humans, after all, but lumping everyone in the same mold diminishes the delightful differences between us. Personality plays a part when it comes to how men and women make and keep friends. Extroverts and introverts show distinct patterns of relating. An introverted woman will develop and maintain friendships differently than an extroverted woman. She will have fewer and probably deeper friendships than the extrovert. But both extroverted and introverted women strongly long for friendship. They need the security of supportive, loving relationships in their lives. The distinction between introverts and extroverts doesn't appear to be as strong for men, although they too will base the number and depth of their friendships on their personality preferences.

In spite of the pressure in recent history to erase differences between men and women, boys and girls, the distinctions remain obvious. How, then, do these differences affect friendship in marriage?

FRIENDSHIP IN MARRIAGE

Marriage is a great venue for practicing friendship. Living in such close proximity with another person, we see all of our spouse's flaws and faults as well as his or her virtues. All the virtuous qualities of a good friendship—intimacy, grace, respect, kindness, patience, fun, and an understanding of the other's priorities—must exist in a growing marriage.

When Jerry's mother died after a sudden and brief bout with cancer, he and his stepfather sat on the couch remembering stories about her. His stepfather said, "Well, the matter is, we got along so well." Not only were they marriage partners, they were best friends. What a compliment to their relationship!

Being good friends with your spouse doesn't mean exclusivity.

Some men have reasoned that they don't need close male friends, saying, "My wife is my best friend and my accountability partner." That may be true, but it also puts pressure on the wife to be his sole support and keeps the husband from benefiting from the support and wisdom of other men. It is legitimate and healthy to be best friends with one's marriage partner but never to the exclusion of other relationships. Marriage partners with an intimate friendship can easily extend friendship to others.

Obviously, not all married couples are good friends. Sometimes the cause of this is too much emphasis on sexual intimacy. Although sexual intimacy is a very important and prominent part of marriage, it should never eclipse the pursuit of a deep friendship that can carry a couple across the times when sex is clearly not enough. (And, by the way, it never is.) Marriage books repeatedly emphasize the need for communication, respect, and care in building the marriage relationship.

Other issues that hinder friendship in marriage include a lack of intellectual and emotional interaction, taking each other for granted, differing values, and living with unresolved conflict. Many couples live at the functional and sexual levels and do not pay attention to the deeper issues of friendship and communication. And when another man or woman listens in a way a spouse does not, a person might be tempted to cross the line to a wrong intimacy that breaks one's marriage vows. We must constantly work on developing friendship inside marriage.

Key to developing a good friendship with your spouse is learning how to communicate with each other. It helps to remember that men tend to listen with a mindset of problem solving or analysis of the information given, and women often listen to gain content and offer understanding.

When we first married, we had no concept of how to communicate with one another effectively. If Mary was relating an event or a problem, she would be very detailed, often going on rabbit trails into little particulars she found interesting and pertinent. Soon Jerry's eyes would glaze over and his mind would wander to other things. This created frustration and misunderstanding for both of us. Finally, we talked it out, and Jerry said, "Just get to the bottom line, and then fill in the details." Now when Mary starts going into too much detail for Jerry, he gently twirls his index finger and she realizes she needs to skip to the bottom line.

Jerry has the opposite communication weakness. He tends to relate major events with one terse sentence, omitting pertinent details. The following dialogue reveals the problem.

Jerry: "I heard that the Smiths had their baby today."

Mary: "Oh, wonderful. What was it, a boy or girl?"

Jerry: "Well, I'm not sure, but I know it was one or the other."

Occasionally when we're talking, Jerry will listen and absorb what Mary is saying but not respond verbally. He's thinking and processing the information. After waiting a few moments, Mary will ask him to at least say, "Uh-huh."

Fortunately, we have made some progress in our way of communicating with each other. It has helped us both to know we are not deliberately frustrating each other with our conversations but rather exhibiting our differences as men and women.

The word "listen" contains the same letters as the word "silent."—Alfred Brendel

---

We have also been greatly helped by learning to listen without interruption. This isn't just important in marriage; it is key in any relationship. At one point in his Air Force career, Jerry had a commander who was an efficient and caring man. His wife showed a most appealing personality trait. She turned her full attention on the person she was with. She listened, responded in ways that showed she understood what was said, and never showed impatience with the other person. Understandably, this woman never lacked for friends. Listening attentively with understanding and caring provides a strong basis for friendship and is essential in marriage.

FRIENDSHIPS BETWEEN THE SEXES

Now we come to a critical question: Is it wise for married men and women to have deep friendships with the opposite sex? The answer is yes and no, which on the surface doesn't sound helpful. There is always the issue of purity of motive and intent in these friendships. Big cautions must be in place when these friendships form to ensure they remain friendships and do not move beyond that.

Shaunti Feldhahn has written two books that provide valuable insight into the differences between men and women: *For Women Only* and, with her husband, *For Men Only*. We asked her about friendships between the sexes, and she expressed that it is difficult — even impossible — to have a *close* friendship with someone of the opposite sex if one of the people is married. More possibilities exist if both are single. Even then, clear boundaries for purity and intent must be established in the minds of both.[2] The following story illustrates why.

A church hired a new music director, who came with high ideals and hopes that he would help people grow in their spiritual lives. He did an excellent job of leading the worship music and attempting to disciple the volunteers in the music program. He spent time coaching the most talented soprano in the choir, often following choir practice when the church was empty. Gradually, this professional relationship grew to a friendship that included sharing disappointments in their marriage partners. Eventually, the music instruction stopped and inappropriate touching began. Within a year, the music director and the soprano married and moved away, leaving five children and two spouses heartbroken and bewildered.

A classic case of friendship gone awry.

Boundaries are crucial in friendship between men and women. Any friendship with the opposite sex requires a commitment to purity and integrity and a determination to offer a friendship that builds up and helps the other person without any expectations or pressure.

In Romans 16, we see that the apostle Paul had deep and lasting friendships with both men and women. He always described his friendships with women in respectful, even brotherly, ways. He emphasized their efforts together in the progress of the gospel. His focus was on the spiritual partnership and friendship.

We have many friends who are single, whether divorced, widowed, or never married. Their need for friendship and companionship is as strong as for any married person. They can experience loneliness in a couples' world. Even though their primary friendships may be of their own gender, they have much to offer and to gain in multigender friendships at work, in social settings, and at church. We must never think that their motive is to find a spouse. They bring a rich dimension and understanding to any friendship.

All of this points to the need for understanding and grace in the friendships we have as men and women. We must make every effort to allow friendship patterns to play out, carefully guarding appropriate boundaries. Men and women can be, and should be, good friends, whether in work or social situations. They can relate well with each other bringing their feminine or masculine perspectives to projects, mission trips, Bible studies, and social settings. In our interviews, many people expressed great appreciation for mixed-gender settings in church and for community projects. Among younger people, there were healthy friendships, encouragement, fun, and camaraderie between the sexes. Paul gave Timothy this wise counsel of friendship: "Treat younger men as brothers, older women as mothers, and younger women as sisters, with absolute purity" (1 Timothy 5:1-2).

COUPLE-TO-COUPLE FRIENDSHIPS

Some of our most significant friendships have been with other couples, not just with individuals, although both kinds of friendship are fulfilling. Couple-to-couple friendships bring an opportunity for fresh perspectives and enjoyment that doesn't exist when husbands and wives have only individual friendships.

Consider this. When two wives are good friends, will the couples socialize? More often than not, the answer is yes. If the husbands are good friends, will the couples socialize? In our research, the answer was almost unanimous: "Likely not." Wives usually drive the social activities in a marriage. But remember, social activities are only one aspect of friendship.

Earlier we spoke of risks that arise in friendships between men and women. The same risk holds true in couple-to-couple relationships. Checks and balances, truthfulness and frankness must be in place as safeguards. One of our close friends told us, "I have no friendships of which my wife is not a part, including my friendships with men. She brings balance and safety and enjoyment to the friendships." By contrast, Jerry has many male friendships of which Mary is only a peripheral part. Mary, likewise, has female friends who Jerry knows but without the deep friendship Mary has. Gifting and personality play a significant part in determining how integrated a husband's and wife's friendships will be.

One of the primary contexts for our friendships with other married people is couples' Bible studies. Having husband and wife in a study together keeps the sharing open and honest. A husband might share some area or issue only to notice a raised eyebrow or glance from his wife to question or correct. Sometimes someone will begin to talk and then ask, "Dear, is it okay to share this?" The advantage of a men-only or women-only group is in talking about deeper issues that would not be easy or appropriate in a mixed group. Both couples' and gender-specific groups are important in the building and sharing of friendships and in stimulating spiritual growth.

In our covenant group, the sharing is open and direct. We often joke with each other about being put on the "hot seat." Being on the hot seat can be uncomfortable, but when we are transparent with each other, it deepens our trust in one another. Being on the hot seat can help us "walk the talk." As we have matured and grown together as friends, there is far less need for the hot seat, and encouragement is more common in our discussions.

In this chapter, we have shared some of the dynamics and differences in the building and developing of friendships for men and women. Of course, every person is unique. We learn those differences and adjust for them in much the same way as we do for personality differences.

THOUGHTS and DISCUSSION

1. Do you agree or disagree with the differences between men and women as described in this chapter? Explain your answer.
2. As you have developed friendships with the opposite gender, what lessons have you learned?
3. List three couples you are friends with and describe how you relate to one another. If you are single, how do you relate to couples?
4. How do the differences in men's and women's friendship styles affect your friendships with people of the opposite sex?

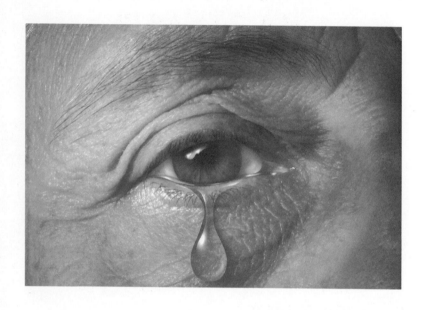

Chapter 10

WHO CARES IF I'M DOWN?

When we honestly ask ourselves which person in our lives means the most to us, we often find that it is those who, instead of giving advice, solutions or cures have chosen rather to share our pain and patch our wounds with a warm and tender hand.

HENRI NOUWEN

The friend in my adversity I shall always cherish most. I can better trust those who helped to relieve the gloom of my dark hours than those who are so ready to enjoy with me the sunshine of my prosperity.

ULYSSES S. GRANT

ULYSSES S. GRANT SUFFERED much. His businesses failed; he started drinking; he was denied employment as an engineer and had to try to make a living in St. Louis by selling firewood. When he attempted to reenter the military at the outbreak of the Civil War, he was rejected. He suffered losses in battle, endured the criticism of Congress, and was plagued by migraine headaches. At age forty-six, he was the youngest man at that time to be elected president of the United States. After serving in the presidency for two terms, he again failed in business. He knew firsthand the story of failure, discouragement, and depression. This gives substance to his statement on friendship at the beginning of this chapter.[1] No one wants a "fair-weather friend," who is there only when all is well.

Fair weather friends, fair weather sailors,
Will leave you stranded on life's shore.
One good friend who truly loves you
Is worth the pain your heart endures.—*Johnny Cash*

Close friendship often has roots in suffering. Where there is suffering, there is depth. The wind that causes some trees to fall causes others to dig their roots into the soil more deeply. What lasts must be tested.

When we walk with our friends in suffering (theirs or ours), the friendship either fades or flourishes. Friendship in suffering derives its source from emotion but more so from commitment. As we walk with a suffering friend, we see the raw cry of need. We either run away or grasp a sweaty, tense hand and hold on for dear life. Sometimes that is all we can do. We simply make ourselves available, and we stand with our friend.

THE FACE OF FRIENDSHIP IN SUFFERING

What does friendship look like when your friend is suffering?

Being There

Rudy Giuliani once said, "Weddings are optional, but funerals are mandatory."[2] Your presence is more important in suffering than during times of joy and laughter. Phone calls, cards, and flowers help, but presence speaks most loudly.

The apostle Paul talked of his need for the presence of a friend. In Macedonia, he was lonely and depressed. He said, "God . . . comforted [me] by the coming of Titus" (2 Corinthians 7:6). Later, when he was in prison, he said to his closest friend, Timothy, "At my first defense, no one came to my support, but everyone deserted me" (2 Timothy 4:16).

When Lazarus died, Jesus came to be with Mary and Martha. The disciples, knowing He could have healed Lazarus, said, "Why bother? He's already dead." But Jesus wanted to be with Mary and Martha in their sorrow. He went anyway, knowing that He needed to "be there." When Jesus arrived, both Mary and Martha upbraided Him for not coming sooner. "If you had been here, my brother would not have died" (John 11:21), Martha said. They wanted Him present before Lazarus's death, thinking His healing power was the only solution (see verses 1-44).

We too know the value of presence in deep suffering. We were traveling when we received the news about our son's death. The three couples in our covenant group immediately boarded planes to come to Colorado Springs to help us. They could have arranged to get help for us, but they dropped everything and came themselves. They took over our lives, handling the media, driving us to appointments, mowing our lawn, shopping for our groceries, cooking and cleaning, helping us think through decisions, planning a memorial service, answering endless phone calls, and serving us in so many ways. Few others could have taken over our lives as these covenant friends did. We had spent years developing these friendships. Our friends had earned the right to enter our lives.

People from our church and The Navigators also helped in countless ways. Two of our Navigator colleagues came to our home at 9:00 a.m. for many days to check on us, to see how we were doing, to help us. They could have called, but they came. Another friend changed the sheets on all the beds in the house and left candy on the pillows — a small, loving gesture to express her care for us in our grief. People "being there" spoke volumes of their love and concern for us.[3]

Some people are intimidated by being in the presence of another who is going through grief, sorrow, or difficulty. They feel awkward, don't know what to say, and feel helpless. Again, we emphasize that a loving presence is what helps most during difficult times. Practical opportunities to help will be apparent, but you have to be there in order to see those possibilities.

Serving

Jesus came to serve, not to be served (see Matthew 20:28). Likewise, when a friend is suffering, we enter his life to serve, expecting nothing in return. We do not give orders or directions. We try to lift our friend's load. When we hear about the quiet suffering of a parent of a teen who is running with the wrong crowd, or a friend suffering disappointment over family tensions, we can serve by listening to that person and praying for and with him. When we hear about someone who has lost a job or has a chronic illness, we can pray, provide counsel, network care for him, share our financial resources, and listen with patience.

Some time ago, we went to visit some close missionary friends. At the last minute, we had filled a sack with food from our pantry and freezer. Later our friends told us how they'd had no food in the house, nothing to serve us, and out of that sack had come a lunch for the four of us. We were unaware of their desperate situation but felt that God directed us to help these friends who were in need.

When someone is suffering physically, his or her needs are usually simple to identify. We take food for the family, visit the hospital, send cards, or care for the children. We can initiate this level of help without being asked. Emotional suffering is far more complex, so it is more difficult to know how to help. Most people are unaware of other people's emotional pain, but the closest of friends see it, and they can more readily help. One mark of a close or intimate friendship is the intuitive sense of what is happening with a friend. When you sense a friend is hurting emotionally, always ask permission to enter that emotional space and help. If you don't, or if you do not have a proven and trusted history with the hurting person, your "help" can feel more like an intrusion.

Let's not think that the suffering must be great or catastrophic before a friend can serve. Friends sense suffering at any level and look for ways to help. We have recorded a number of practical suggestions for how to help those who are suffering in *Harsh Grief, Gentle Hope*.

A WORD ABOUT FAMILY

One reason for developing and enriching family friendships is that they become the first line of defense in times of suffering. In some parts of our U.S. culture and around the world, relationships and friendships inside the family supersede all other friendships. In societies where family structures have been diminished or are broken, the family may not be there to help. When suffering hits, a healthy family is most aware, understands the need, and can most appropriately step in to help. Family—especially parents, children, brothers and sisters—should be at the frontline of help in difficult times: "Anyone who won't care for his own relatives when they need help, especially those living in his own family, has no right to say he is a Christian" (1 Timothy 5:8, TLB).

THE TWO SIDES OF HELP IN SUFFERING

Most of us readily step up to serve a friend in times of suffering or difficulty, but do we permit others to step into our lives at such times? Sometimes it is more difficult to receive help than to give help. This is especially true for people who have been strong, independent, generous, and capable all their lives. However, there will come times when we must swallow our pride and ask for and receive help. Certainly as we get older we will all find ourselves in this position. When we do, we need to ask for help. That's what Elijah did.

The Old Testament prophet Elijah was a fearsome and courageous man. He faced down King Ahab and his scheming wife, Jezebel. After confronting Ahab, he fled for his life. When he was about to starve, he had to ask for help from a widow in the small town of Zarephath. She was also starving from the drought and famine that Elijah had predicted. Elijah asked, "Would you bring me a little water in a jar so I may have a drink?" And then, "And bring me, please, a piece of bread" (1 Kings 17:10-11). It was a simple request, but the widow said that she had only a handful of flour and a little oil that she and her son would eat and then die. Elijah told her not to be afraid and that if she would feed him, the flour and oil would not be used up. By faith, she did, and she saved Elijah and her family. Elijah had to ask for and receive help.

We need to do the same. Suffering is not just illness or death but includes events such as bankruptcies, divorce, loss of job, economic difficulties, academic failures, children's rebellion, children's ill health, and relational conflicts. In each of these situations, friends are in the best position to be aware of the need and enter into our lives. We need to be willing to allow people to help and serve in loving and practical ways.

MODELING VIRTUE

As we enter into the life of someone who is suffering, we model virtue and virtuous friendship. We serve, expecting nothing in return. Our presence and our actions speak loudly. Most of us gladly serve our friends, but we must also serve people beyond our friendship circles as we become aware of needs and are led by God to help.

When we do, our serving can lead to friendship. Many times we have become friends with those who have stepped in to help us. Similarly, we have become friends with those we have helped. This has been particularly true with people who have lost a child, as we have.

One of the most striking of the hundreds of anecdotes of Abraham Lincoln's life is one that tells of his being at the bedside of a dying soldier during the Civil War. "Are you really my president?" asked the soldier. "Yes," Lincoln replied. Lincoln then wrote a letter to the soldier's mother at the young man's dictation. Then the soldier asked, "Won't you stay with me? I do want to hold on to your hand." And Lincoln did.[4] May we never neglect to be there and hold a hand.

THOUGHTS and DISCUSSION

1. How has suffering entered into your friendships?
2. Describe a time when you were discouraged and a friend entered into your life to help you.
3. Why do some friendships suffer when one of the friends is emotionally low? Which friends (from the Circle of Friendships on page 35) are most likely to enter your life?
4. Where does your family fit when you are discouraged?

Chapter 11

BROKEN OR DAMAGED FRIENDSHIPS

It's tough when someone special starts to ignore you, but it's even tougher to pretend you don't mind.

LEE MAO FEY

Friendship is like a glass ornament. Once it is broken, it can rarely be put back together exactly the same way.

CHARLES KINGSLEY

What are these wounds on your body? . . . The wounds I was given at the house of my friends.

ZECHARIAH 13:6

RELATIONSHIPS ARE FRAGILE. They weather some storms, not others. People slight each other. They wound each other. These slights and wounds are not always intentional, but even so, a mis-spoken word or misunderstanding can break the bonds of a good friendship. When a friendship is broken, it does not mean that the friendship is gone but rather that some of the threads that have formed the bonds of friendship have been damaged. We have all experienced that uncomfortable tension when we know the tone of the friendship has changed. Calls stop. A coolness or indifference develops. The more obvious and hurtful breaks typically come from a direct conflict or argument.

The apostle Paul and his close friend Barnabas experienced such a break. Barnabas wanted Mark to accompany them for a return trip to visit churches they had planted. Paul, remembering a disappointing experience with Mark, did not want him included. Paul and Barnabas "had such a sharp disagreement that they parted company" (Acts 15:39). This must have been incredibly painful. We hear nothing more of Barnabas in the New Testament. We do not know if the two ever reconciled. Scripture gives no indication of who was right in this dispute.

Churches and congregations have been damaged and split as a result of conflict between members. This is a sad reality. Both sides claim to love Jesus and desire His kingdom to advance. Often pride interferes and neither side is willing to give in. However, there are biblical means of walking through these difficult times. In this chapter, we will primarily talk about individual friendships and reconciliation. Impact on the broader community and ways of healing is addressed well in Ken Sande's book *The Peacemaker*.[1]

THE CAUSES OF BROKEN FRIENDSHIPS

As frail humans, we always have enough blame to go around. We need to be specific and name some of the causes of broken friendships.

Betrayal

According to *Merriam-Webster's*, to betray someone is to "act with treachery or disloyalty, to violate a confidence." King David experienced this pain: "This friend of mine betrayed me—I who was at peace with him. He broke his promises. His words were oily smooth, but in his heart was war. His words were sweet, but underneath were daggers" (Psalm 55:20-21, TLB). The person he was referring to here was likely Ahithophel, who claimed to be David's friend while he was plotting to help Absalom, David's son, take over the kingship.

When we are betrayed, the way forward is often murky. Matthew 18:15 guides us in what to do: "If your brother or sister sins, go and point out their fault, just between the two of you. If they listen to you, you have won them over." The remainder of this passage describes what to do if your friend doesn't listen. This is a difficult process at best. There is a difference in a malicious, deliberate betrayal and when the other person did not intend or understand the action as a betrayal. What you see as a betrayal may, in your friend's eyes, be just a mistake or a lapse of judgment. In either case, you need healing, and your friend needs forgiveness. If you continue to bear a grudge or remain angry, you will not heal, nor will the friendship. Delayed action will only make reconciliation more difficult.

Betrayal violates every concept of loyalty, one of the foundational elements of friendship. In the secular world and in political intrigues, betrayal is common. It should not be so in a world of Jesus followers.

Spoken Words

Do you remember the childhood rhyme "Sticks and stones may break my bones, but words will never hurt me"? Nothing could be further from the truth. Most friendships break over unkind or harsh words. Words sink into our minds, invade our dreams, and threaten our self-esteem. Carole Mayhall beautifully addresses the need for discretion in her book *Words That Hurt, Words That Heal*.

Discretion means the quality of being careful or discreet about what one does and says. Discreet, in turn, means to be prudent, tactful, judicious, cautious, circumspect, diplomatic, and polite. . . . Discretion is knowing when to speak and when to be quiet. — Carole Mayhall

We can speak truth to people, but it must be in love. When a wife asks her husband, "How do you like this dress?" he must use caution in answering. One of our daughters once asked Jerry this question about a new skirt she was wearing. He thoughtlessly replied, "I think you should burn it." He is still apologizing for that mistake! We need to choose our words carefully, as they have great power.

Careless words, jokes, and criticisms slip out so easily. Those who are "quick with the lip" in retorts and jokes may need to be especially careful. Years ago, Jerry attended a retreat at an Air Force base chapel. In casual conversation, he made a joke about a mode of baptism. He offended the chaplain's assistant, as that type of baptism was no joke to him. Jerry apologized, but the damage was done.

Again and again, the Bible warns about the power of the tongue:

It only takes a spark, remember, to set off a forest fire. A careless or wrongly placed word out of your mouth can do that. By our speech we can ruin the world, turn harmony to chaos, throw mud on a reputation, send the whole world up in smoke and go up in smoke with it, smoke right from the pit of hell. (James 3:5-7, MSG)

The words of the reckless pierce like swords, but the tongue of the wise brings healing. (Proverbs 12:18)

Those who guard their mouths and their tongues keep themselves from calamity. (21:23)

Words hurt. Because of this, the two of us have adopted a new way of diverting conflict in our relationship by one of us saying, "You may be right." That statement allows both of us to step back, take a breath, and avoid harsh words. It leaves both of us with some dignity in the conflict and brings space to see another point of view.

Sin

Sin in your life or a friend's life can shatter the friendship. For example, when one of our friends decided to leave his wife for another woman, we had no choice but to confront him and disrupt the friendship. He left his wife and remarried. Our relationship with him was never restored. Another friend was caught up in pornography. He acknowledged his addiction, told Jerry about it, and received help. Consequently, the friendship deepened and grew.

Subtle sins can also be devastating to a friendship. Pride, ego, and ambition change how we act toward our friends. Proverbs states it bluntly: "Pride leads to conflict" (Proverbs 13:10, NLT). Jerry was talking with friends during a time when he had a pressing schedule. He felt impatient. They sensed it and felt that he thought his time was more important than theirs. He apologized and settled in to enjoy his friends. Fortunately, they extended grace and forgiveness to him for his distraction and impatience.

Jealousy and envy can also destroy friendships. We rarely find equality in possessions or status. Jealousy due to inequality can be a barrier to forming friendships, and it can be the cause of the breakdown of a friendship.

This was the case for Janet and Melinda, who were best friends in college. Both married, and the friendship continued. Then their husbands' careers developed differently. Janet's husband had a good job, but it was negatively affected by the falling economy. Melinda's husband entered an industry where there was growth. He rapidly gained a promotion and significant wealth. Janet and her husband struggled, living frugally in a modest home. Melinda and her husband bought a new home, a lake house, a boat, and other expensive items. Soon their social circles began to differ and they did fewer things together. Ultimately, the friendship failed. Both had inner issues that hurt the friendship: Janet felt embarrassed and a bit jealous, and Melinda flaunted her newfound wealth.

Comparison is deadly. If we compare ourselves to others who are struggling when we are experiencing success, we can become proud and arrogant. When we understand that our success is temporary and under God's direction, we are humble and can use the opportunities we are given to bless others. If we compare ourselves to others who are experiencing success when we're struggling, we open ourselves to envy and jealousy. When we rejoice in another's success, whether a good marriage or having successful children or financial achievement, we are blessed. No matter the issues, we need to guard our hearts and protect the true basis of friendship.

Conflict

Minor and major conflicts are part of life's reality. The sources and causes of conflicts vary widely. Misspoken words, differences of opinion, and arguments bring tension that leads to cruel words that cannot be reclaimed. When you see conflict coming, be sure to count the cost of letting it develop.

Anger and misunderstandings can break friendships. Most of us deal with some level of anger in our lives. When we express it outwardly in words and actions, it quickly escalates and can be destructive. Anger turned inward affects our attitudes and ability to be whole in our friendships. When you sense anger rising in yourself, you first need to deal with it and let it settle. If you need to express something that angered you to a friend, do so with care, gentleness, and humility. If you realize there has been a misunderstanding between you and a friend, you can most likely address it through a simple conversation.

Differences of opinion come into play whether we're playing

sports, talking about politics, or discussing child rearing, doctrine, or business, so anticipate them. Let iron sharpen iron (see Proverbs 27:17). Learn to disagree agreeably. Allow others to express themselves. Respect their opinion. There will be times when it is best not to voice your contrary opinion. In the earlier stages of relationships, try not to be provocative or combative, even if you don't agree. We have found that in political discussions, it is often better to say nothing than to engage in arguments. You might wonder if the friendship is real if such matters cannot be discussed. Friendship does not mean agreeing on everything; it means giving room for our friends to have different views. We can discuss without rancor and anger and even agree to disagree. The relationship is more important than our opinion.

HEALING AND RESTORATION

The guiding scriptural passage for healing and restoration is "Make every effort to live in peace with everyone and to be holy. . . . See to it that no one falls short of the grace of God and that no bitter root grows up to cause trouble and defile many" (Hebrews 12:14-15). If you have a friendship that needs restoration, the responsibility rests primarily on you, not the other person. Remember, we are discussing healing and restoration between friends, not the world in general. It is always your move. The healing process requires humility and patience. The other person bears responsibility too, but you can be responsible for only yourself.

It may be that the hurt and betrayal is so strong that friendship restoration is impossible. The broken trust is too deep to recover. Even so, try to reach a point of understanding and forgiveness while letting the friendship go.

The first step in any healing is seeing the need, identifying the problem. You may know there is a problem in a relationship but not know why. If so, use what we've discussed in this chapter so far to help you identify the cause of the break. Or approach your friend and say, "I know we have had a bit of tension. Do you remember what might have caused this to happen?"

Once you identify the issue, take some time to pray about it. Write some notes to clarify your thinking. When Jerry is in conflict, he doesn't sleep well. In his half-awake state, all kinds of emotions plague him. Usually none of the thoughts is rational. Writing out your thoughts gives you the opportunity to create a realistic solution. It can also help to write out what you will say when you talk to your friend. Matthew 5:24 tells us, "First go and be reconciled to them; then come and offer your gift." Every reconciliation requires forgiveness on the part of both parties. Be willing to take the first step, even if it means rejection. We want peace, certainly, but we also want to restore the friendship.

Restoration is easiest when the offense is recent. "Get rid of all bitterness, rage and anger, brawling and slander, along with every form of malice. Be kind and compassionate to one another, forgiving each other, just as in Christ God forgave you" (Ephesians 4:31-32). A person who has brooded for weeks or months over a matter might attempt to correct it with tight lips and clenched fists. If the offense is faced quickly, it is much easier to approach a friend with kind words and a steady tongue.

When you seek reconciliation and forgiveness, go in an attitude of humility. Once you have discussed why the conflict occurred and are ready to initiate restoration, talk privately with your friend. It should be in a comfortable setting and at a time and place where you won't be interrupted or have time constraints. Some people find it difficult to ask for forgiveness without excusing their bad behavior or unkind words. Decide beforehand to accept responsibility for the conflict.

If you have been hurt by a friend, you might say to him or her something like, "Yesterday when we were having lunch, you made jokes about our daughter. I know you meant well, but it still hurt, particularly because our daughter has been working through some issues and is growing. I don't want our friendship to be threatened by things like that."

If you sense that you have said or done something that gave offense, you could say, "Lately I've felt uncomfortable about our friendship. Our conversation seems to be strained. Have I offended you in any way? If I have, I really want to make it right and have your forgiveness."

An apology is a friendship preserver, an antidote for hatred, never a sign of weakness; it costs nothing but one's pride, always saves more than it costs, and is a device needed in every home. — *unknown*

Unfortunately, even when attempts are made, some friendships never return to their original closeness. They are like a metal paper clip that has been straightened; you can never get it back to its original state, as it will always have a bit of a kink. (See for yourself: Take a metal paper clip. Unbend it. Try to straighten it. Now bend one of the straight parts sharply. Straighten it. What happens?) Similarly, some friendships never go back to what they were. When they are bent or damaged, a memory remains. We wish it were different, as ideally every relationship is capable of mending. The biblical requirement is to resolve the conflict, not necessarily restore the depth of friendship.

Friendship is fragile. Handle with care.

THOUGHTS and DISCUSSION

1. Describe one of your broken friendships (not a romantic one). How did the break affect you?

2. Look at the list of the ways friendships are broken (see pages 124–128). Which do you think is the most prevalent?
3. How does sin impact a friendship?
4. When a friendship breaks due to something other than moral failure, how do you identify and address the cause?
5. Describe and discuss your experience with forgiveness, healing, and restoration.

Chapter 12

LET'S PARTY!

Mirth is God's medicine. Everybody ought to bathe in it.

HENRY WARD BEECHER

What soap is to the body, laughter is to the soul.

YIDDISH PROVERB

LASTING FRIENDSHIPS NEED MOMENTS — sometimes hours and days — of lightness, laughter, frivolity, and fun. Whether the friendship is between two people or a group, fun should be an integral part. But if it's the dominant feature, the friendship may remain shallow.

Fun has a broad, subjective meaning. Some folks are party animals, while others are somber and quiet. People describe their ideas of fun in many ways: amusement, recreation, adventure, travel, entertainment, play. What might be fun to one person alarms or repels another. After a day of mountain biking, one man said, "Wasn't that terrific?" but his wife said, "Never again!" She faced a trail so steep that she almost somersaulted her bike. Her husband loved the challenge and the risk. She would have preferred browsing in the small, historical museum in the town at the beginning of the bike trail followed by a few hours of shopping. Different people, different preferences.

So look for common ground when searching for fun things to do with friends. Compromises may be needed. Trial and error helps you discover shared interests and activities.

The first time Jerry asked Mary for a date, he asked if she would like to play tennis. She said yes. Jerry was surprised to find himself chasing balls that regularly sailed over the fence. Finally, he asked if she knew how to play. Mary said, "No, but you didn't ask me that. You asked if I would *like* to play tennis." Later in our marriage, Jerry gave Mary a gift certificate for tennis lessons. Again, the balls went every which way except over the net into the opposing court. We finally decided that tennis was a fun activity we would never share. We needed to explore some other avenues of mutual enjoyment.

With that said, let's look at some ways you can bring more fun into your friendships.

ALLOW FOR SPONTANEITY

Fun and fellowship doesn't need to be the same in every circumstance. Add some spontaneity to the mix.

We were with a group of eight friends, enjoying lunch at one of the friend's homes on a beautiful spring day near the beach. The conversation was delightful, varying between serious topics and laughter about frivolous things. After dessert, the hostess suddenly commanded, "Into the cars, everyone." Surprised, we followed her instructions and ended up on a hillside above the beach. She handed kites to all of us. Most of us hadn't flown a kite for twenty years or more. We spent two hours launching and sailing our kites in the spring wind. That afternoon has remained fresh in our minds, much more so than an afternoon of watching television or even talking would have.

Another time, this same friend gathered the same small group together. Instead of preparing dinner, she suggested we all go to the local deli, spend ten dollars on a sandwich and drink of our choice, and go to a nearby park to eat. We took blankets, sat on the grass, and ate together. As dusk fell, our friend passed out books to each one and we read poetry to one another. When it became dark, she handed small candles to everyone to give light and warmth to our little circle. We made another memory to treasure.

When our children were young, we would arrange spur-of-the-moment slumber parties for our children's friends and their families. The children brought sleeping bags and slept in a jumble on the living room floor while the parents searched for available beds. Meals were improvised and everyone enjoyed being together as our friendships deepened.

SHARE SOME QUIET MOMENTS

There's a story told of early Scandinavian settlers on the barren Midwest prairies in the nineteenth century. One couple would drive their horse and wagon to the next farmhouse and they would sit in companionable silence for the evening drinking coffee and watching the fireplace. As they prepared to leave, they would tell the hosts, "We had a wonderful time. So fun to be with you."

Fun doesn't always have to include "doing" something. It can be subdued, quiet moments sharing a peaceful activity such as listening to favorite music, reading in companionable silence, or discussing a book or a current-event topic.

We recently spent three days with close friends at a Southern California resort. We spent much time talking but also enjoyed long periods of silence while each of us read. Those quiet moments reflected the comfort, relaxation, and acceptance we feel when we're together.

Constant chatter can diminish the fun. Quietness can increase it. This is particularly true in times of severe grief, stress, sadness, and worry. If a friend is suffering in some way, urging him or her to do something fun may simply cause further discouragement. An old proverb says, "Even in laughter the heart may ache, and rejoicing may end in grief" (Proverbs 14:13). Quiet encouragement to a friend in pain offers much better solace than raucous fun.

LAUGH TOGETHER

Recent studies in the field of gelotology (the benefits of laughter) have proven the valuable effects of laughter on the human body. In her book *A Better Brain at Any Age*, Sondra Kornblatt wrote that laughter:

- Lowers blood pressure
- Increases vascular blood flow and oxygenation of the blood
- Gives a workout to the diaphragm and abdominal, respiratory, facial, leg, and back muscles
- Reduces certain stress hormones such as cortisol and adrenaline
- Increases the response of tumor and disease-killing cells
- Defends against respiratory infections
- Increases memory and learning
- Improves alertness, creativity, and memory[1]

Laughter not only benefits us physically but also lightens our emotions and brings welcome distraction from the ordinary stresses of the day. When our son died, we couldn't imagine ever laughing again. Every day was a heavy, painful episode to get through. Three weeks after his death, we met with close friends for a few days at a mountain resort. We thought we might be a somber influence on the weekend with our ever-present grief, but to our amazement, when one of our friends said something funny, we laughed with the same exuberance as our friends. We almost felt we had betrayed our grief, but with the sympathy and caring of our friends, that laughter gave us hope that eventually normalcy would return to our lives.

This experience would not have had the same value with strangers, but laughter with close friends brought hope for healing.

Laughter is an instant vacation. — *Milton Berle*

In his book *Anatomy of an Illness*, Norman Cousins told how he suffered a stroke and initiated laughter-producing activities to contribute to his healing. He wrote,

> We began the part of the program calling for full exercise of the affirmative emotions as a factor in enhancing body chemistry. It was easy enough to hope and love and have faith, but what about laughter? Nothing is less funny than being flat on your back with all the bones in your spine and joints hurting. A systematic program was indicated. A good place to begin, I thought, was with amusing movies. Allen Funt, producer of the spoofing television program "Candid Camera," sent films of some of his CC classics along with a projector. We were even able to get our hands on some old Marx brothers' films. It worked. I made the joyous discovery that ten minutes of genuine belly laughter had an anesthetic effect and would give me at least two hours of pain-free sleep.[2]

You may not be flat on your back with pain, but you may need the same release and refreshing that comes from laughter. Whether we're in a happy mood or suffering, laughter lifts our spirits and brings a joyous aspect to life. It makes us ready to be a better friend.

PLAN FUN ACTIVITIES

Too often, friends rely on the old standard of going to the movies or watching TV. That is fine periodically but not as a steady diet of entertainment. When two, four, six, or more friends are sitting side by side staring at moving images on a screen, relating isn't typically part of the equation. However, there is no specific rule, and watching an old, familiar movie on a DVD with friends can be relaxing. We have good memories of watching the Robin Williams movie *RV* with friends. We owned an RV at the time, so we laughed till our sides ached. Another time, we gathered our extended family with grandchildren to watch the original movie version of *Les Misérables*. We paused the recording periodically to discuss what the movie meant. That evening is still a treasured family memory from one of our many movie nights.

People who aren't particularly creative in proposing fun activities can watch and learn from friends who are or consult the Internet or the library for ideas. Fun doesn't have to be expensive. It can be free or low-budget, saving costly fun for occasional times. When looking for enjoyable activities, find things to do that are active rather than passive. Here are a few ideas to get you started:

- Take a blanket to a park or lake, bring books of poetry or jokes, and share laughter or thoughtful ideas.
- Invite friends for dinner, have small pizza crusts ready along with toppings, and have everyone make their own. This is especially enjoyable when new friends are involved, as it's easier to converse while involved in an activity.
- Learn a new card game that requires interaction. Solitaire won't do!
- Attach the computer to the TV and look at old photos and videos. Interaction and laughter guaranteed!
- Explore historical museums in your area. Some of these are tiny but fascinating and often free.
- Look for other free activities in your area—parades, sports, concerts—and plan an outing around the chosen activity.
- Take a walk, place a few pennies on a railroad track, and check the result after a train passes.

- Make a short video of friends telling of an embarrassing moment. Play it back and wait for the laughter.
- Ice skate if your ankles can take it. This is definitely an experience of "friend helping friend."
- Have a Holy Spirit potluck: Bring whatever you're moved to bring. On one occasion, we had six salads and some beans! A healthy meal, to be sure.
- Play a new game. Games of all kinds always produce fun. They can be as slow moving as croquet or as vigorous as touch football. Also try card games, board games, and charades.
- Go to a minor league baseball game.
- Try rafting or, for the more timid, riding a river float.
- Play Frisbee golf. Don't know how? Check the Internet for instructions.

Always remember that fun thrives on interaction, the more the better.

Make fun a significant part of every friendship. We think God is pleased when He hears laughter and joy from the people He created. The psalmist said, "How good and pleasant it is when God's people live together in unity" (Psalm 133:1). One rarely finds division, disagreements, and belligerence where there is laughter and fun. Bring it on!

THOUGHTS and DISCUSSION

1. Recall the last time you experienced genuine laughter. Was it today, yesterday?
2. Create two fun ideas to use with your friends, activities never before tried.
3. How important is laughter to you and why?
4. What place does fun have in your friendships?

CONCLUSION

The last and final word is this: Fear God. Do what he tells you. And that's it. Eventually God will bring everything that we do out into the open and judge it according to its hidden intent, whether it's good or evil.

ECCLESIASTES 12:13-14 (MSG)

THE BOTTOM LINE OF our lives will not be how many friends we made, how we were honored, what we accomplished, or our status or position. In human terms, it will be the quality of our relationships with family and friends.

An underlying assumption undergirds all the principles and instructions throughout this book. This assumption, simply stated, is that Jesus Christ has transformed your life in a personal encounter with Him in salvation. When we speak of virtuous or sacrificial friendship, no event in history compares with Jesus' death on a cross for our sins and His offer of salvation by faith in Him through God's grace: "For it is by grace you have been saved, through faith—and this is not from yourselves, it is the gift of God—not by works, so that no one can boast" (Ephesians 2:8-9). The ultimate relationship and friendship is our relationship to God. "Since our friendship with God was restored by the death of his Son while we were still his enemies, we will certainly be saved through the life of his Son. So now we can rejoice in our wonderful new relationship with God because our Lord Jesus Christ has made us friends of God" (Romans 5:10-11, NLT).

If you are struggling in your friendships, first examine your own friendship with God. As a believer, a follower of Jesus, you have the foundation and power to offer and receive friendship in a unique way. This is not to say that those who are not followers of Jesus cannot experience good friendships. They can. But they will be hindered in both motivation and power.

Being a believer is not a panacea for good friendships. Our friendships will mature and develop as our committed walk with God grows and develops. When we are born, we embark on a lifetime of growth and learning. It is the same for followers of Jesus. Salvation must be followed by spiritual growth both in the knowledge and application of Scripture.

Reflecting on human friendship, we have learned some simple truths:

- We cannot earn someone's friendship. It is given.
- We do not offer conditional friendship, but we give it virtuously.
- A true, virtuous friendship has its roots in relationship with God.
- None of us is a perfect friend, nor can we expect to have perfect friends.
- Our human friendships are frail and vulnerable.
- We must give and receive grace in all our friendships.

As you wrestle with the descriptions in our circles of friendship, realize that friendships are far more complex than these simple illustrations can describe. We hope you will agree, or even disagree, with some of our ideas. But, beyond that, we want you to have taken significant steps to deepen and enhance your friendships.

A key foundation for relationships is found in Romans 12:9-18. Eugene Peterson, in *The Message*, phrases it powerfully:

> Love from the center of who you are; don't fake it. Run for dear life from evil; hold on for dear life to good. Be good friends who love deeply; practice playing second fiddle.
>
> Don't burn out; keep yourselves fueled and aflame. Be alert servants of the Master, cheerfully expectant. Don't quit in hard times; pray all the harder. Help needy Christians; be inventive in hospitality.
>
> Bless your enemies; no cursing under your breath. Laugh with your happy friends when they're happy; share tears when they're down. Get along with each other; don't be stuck-up. Make friends with nobodies; don't be the great somebody.
>
> Don't hit back; discover beauty in everyone. If you've got it in you, get along with everybody.

We aren't to fake friendship. As friends, we are to love deeply. Make friends with ordinary people, nobodies. We can do this only when our lives are being transformed by God. Abraham was called the friend of God, one with whom God spoke face-to-face. We have that same privilege and access to God today, through Jesus Christ.

THOUGHTS and DISCUSSION

1. What were your major friendship lessons as you read this book?
2. What has changed in your view or your practice of friendship? Have you changed?
3. Write down the names of five of your friends. What do you want to change or develop with each of them?
4. What is the most fun aspect of your friendships?

NOTES

Chapter 1: Friends Matter

1. William C. Newton, as quoted in Bill Newton Jr., "More Than Brothers," *Chicken Soup for the Veteran's Soul: Stories to Stir the Pride and Honor the Courage of Our Veterans*, eds. Jack Canfield, Mark Victor Hansen, and Sidney R. Slagter (Deerfield Beach, FL: Health Communications, Inc., 2001), 188–191.
2. Paul Tournier, quoted in Scott Grant, "The Mess of Marriage" (sermon, Peninsula Bible Church, Palo Alto, CA, July 4, 2004), http://www.pbc.org/system/message_files/12388/4872.html.

Chapter 2: Making Friends

1. Laura Schroff and Alex Tresniowski, *An Invisible Thread: The True Story of an 11-Year-Old Panhandler, a Busy Sales Executive, and an Unlikely Meeting with Destiny* (Nashville: Howard Books, 2011).

Chapter 3: The Lego Factor: Building Close Friendships

1. Rudyard Kipling, "A Thousandth Man," *Kipling: A Selection of His Stories and Poems*, ed. John Beecroft (New York: Doubleday, 1956).

Chapter 4: Virtuous Friendship

1. William J. Bennett, *The Book of Virtues: A Treasury of Great Moral Stories* (New York: Simon & Schuster, 1993).
2. Leadership Ministries Worldwide, *Practical Word Studies in the New Testament*, WORDsearch Bible, www.wordsearchbible .com, s.v., n.p.
3. Barbara Petro, "The Nature of Virtuous Friendships," Yahoo! Contributor Network, November 7, 2006, accessed March 7, 2013 http://voices.yahoo.com/the-nature-virtuous-friendships -10264.html.
4. Bennett, 269.
5. Bennett, 270.

Chapter 5: Understanding Each Other

1. For more information about the enneagram, we recommend, Richard Rohr and Andreas Ebert, *The Enneagram: A Christian Perspective* (New York: Crossroad, 2002).
2. For more information on the Myers-Briggs Type Indicator, we recommend Isabel Briggs Myers and Katharine Briggs, *Gifts Differing: Understanding Personality Types* (Mountain View, CA: CPP Inc., 1980, 1995).
3. Stephen Schwartz (music and lyrics), "For Good," Wicked, in Winnie Holzman, A New Musical WICKED: The Untold Story of the Witches of Oz (2009).
4. Margery Williams, *The Velveteen Rabbit* (New York: George H. Doran, 1922).

Chapter 9: Men and Women: Any Difference?

1. Betty MacDonald, *The Egg and I* (New York: Harper & Row, 1945), 211–212.
2. Shaunti Feldhahn, phone interview with the author, May 7, 2013.

Chapter 10: Who Cares If I'm Down?

1. "Ulysses S. Grant," The Biography Channel website, accessed May 18, 2013, http://www.biography.com/people/ulysses-s-grant-9318285.
2. Rudolph W. Giuliani, *Leadership* (New York: Hyperion, 2002).
3. For the full story, see Mary White, *Harsh Grief, Gentle Hope* (Colorado Springs, CO: NavPress, 1994).
4. Recorded in a number of places but one is J. E. Gallaher, *Best Lincoln Stories Tersely Told* (Chicago: M. A. Donohue & Co., 1898). Another source was the *Indianapolis Journal*. It phrased it, "Hold my hand and see me through."

Chapter 11: Broken or Damaged Friendships

1. Ken Sande, *The Peacemaker: A Biblical Guide to Resolving Personal Conflict* (Ada, MI: Baker, 2004).

Chapter 12: Let's Party!

1. Sondra Kornblatt, *A Better Brain at Any Age: The Holistic Way to Improve your Memory, Reduce Stress, and Sharpen Your Wits* (San Francisco: Conari Press, 2009), 42–43.
2. Norman Cousins, *Anatomy of an Illness: As Perceived by the Patient* (New York: Norton, 1979), 39.

ABOUT THE AUTHORS

JERRY WHITE, international president emeritus of The Navigators, is a popular speaker at conferences and seminars. He received a bachelor of science in electrical engineering from the University of Washington and a PhD in astronautics from Purdue University. Dr. White served as a mission controller at Cape Canaveral, was an associate professor at the U.S. Air Force Academy, and retired from the Air Force in 1997 as a major general.

He is the author of several books, including *Rules to Live By*, *The Joseph Road*, *Dangers Men Face*, *Making Peace with Reality*, and *Honesty, Morality, and Conscience*.

MARY WHITE was born in Minnesota, studied creative writing at the University of Washington, and graduated from the University of Colorado. She has been a speaker at many conferences. Together with Jerry, she has written several books and is the author of *Harsh Grief, Gentle Hope*. She and Jerry have four children and eleven grandchildren and live in Colorado Springs, Colorado.

More great books from Jerry and Mary White!

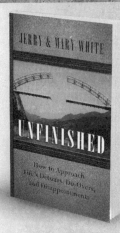

Unfinished
Jerry and Mary White

Jerry and Mary White know from experience that redemption is never out of the question and God is never done. The best way to focus on areas of unfinished work in your life is through the lens of Scripture and encouragement. Gain perspective on your past and find hope for the journey ahead.

978-1-61291-268-4

Rules to Live By
Jerry White

Taken from his years in the military, at NASA, and with The Navigators, Jerry White shares insights and wisdom to point you toward a more balanced life. His fifty-two guiding principles do more than just tell you what you should do — they outline the godly life you can have today.

978-1-60006-270-4

Available wherever books are sold.

NAVPRESS

Discipleship Inside Out®

NAVESSENTIALS

Voices of The Navigators—Past, Present, and Future

NAVESSENTIALS offer core Navigator messages from such authors as Jim Downing, LeRoy Eims, Mike Treneer, and more — at an affordable price. This new series will deeply influence generations in the movement of discipleship. Learn from the old and new messages of The Navigators how powerful and transformational the life of a disciple truly is.

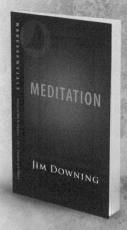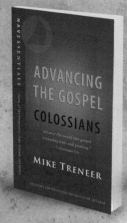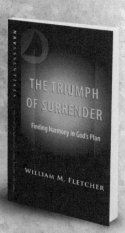

Meditation
by Jim Downing
9781615217250 | $5.00

Advancing the Gospel
by Mike Treneer
9781617471575 | $5.00

The Triumph of Surrender
by William M. Fletcher
9781615219070 | $5.00

Available wherever books are sold.

SUPPORT THE MINISTRY OF THE NAVIGATORS

The Navigators' calling is to advance the gospel of Jesus and His kingdom into the nations through spiritual generations of laborers living and discipling among the lost.

Navigators have invested their lives in people for more than 75 years, coming alongside them life on life to help them passionately know Christ and to make Him known.

The U.S. Navigators' ministry touches lives in varied settings, including college campuses, military bases, downtown offices, urban neighborhoods, prisons, and youth camps.

Dedicated to helping people navigate spiritually, The Navigators aims to make a permanent difference in the lives of people around the world. The Navigators helps its communities of friends to follow Christ passionately and equip them effectively to go out and do the same.

To learn more about donating to The Navigators' ministry, go to **www.navigators.org/us/support** or call toll-free at **1-866-568-7827**.